THE GREATEST BATTLE IN HISTORY...

The events of Sunday, 18 June 1815 have made it perhaps the single most documented and discussed day in world history. Thousands of books have been written about the events that occurred, and the flow shows no sign of abating. Surprising though it may seem, despite all the attention that the Battle of Waterloo has received, there are aspects of it that are not widely known and some that remain unresolved.

Take, for instance, the actions of the 2nd Rocket Troop, Royal Horse Artillery. Because Wellington viewed military rockets as 'nonsense', their effectiveness has been dismissed by many historians. Yet there is evidence that they played a greater role in the battle than is usually acknowledged.

The capture of two French Imperial Eagles are among the most famous incidents during the battle, yet exactly who captured the Eagle of the 105e *Régiment de Ligne* remains unclear. Equally famous is the defeat of Napoleon's Imperial Guard towards the end of the battle by the British 1st Regiment of Guards. As a tribute to their success in repelling the Grenadiers of the Imperial Guard, the British 1st Guards were granted the title Grenadier Guards, a name they proudly bear to this day. Yet it is a fact that the 1st Guards did not defeat the French Grenadiers alone, but others contributed to an even greater extent.

There is also the subject of Wellington's official Waterloo Despatch. This document has formed the basis of every subsequent history of the battle. Yet it is limited in its factual content, considerably diminishing the contribution of the Prussians, without whom the battle could not have been won.

Space, though, does not permit a highly detailed description of every aspect of the battle. Instead we have concentrated on a number of key decisions and actions that brought about the defeat of the Emperor Napoleon and the end of one of history's most turbulent eras. As Victor Hugo declared, 'Waterloo was not a battle but a change in the direction of the world.'

John Grehan

John Grehan - Editor

PREVIOUSLY PUBLISHED 2015
ISBN: 978 1 80282 780 4
Editor: John Greehan
Senior Editor, Bookazines and Specials: Roger Mortimer
Email: roger.mortimer@keypublishing.com
Cover Design: Steve Donovan
Design: Dan Jarman
Advertising Sales Manager: Brodie Baxter
Email: brodie.baxter@keypublishing.com
Tel: 01780 755131
Advertising Production: Debi McGowan
Email: debi.mcgowan@keypublishing.com

SUBSCRIPTION/MAIL ORDER
Key Publishing Ltd, PO Box 300, Stamford, Lincs, PE9 1NA
Tel: 01780 480404
Subscriptions email: subs@keypublishing.com
Mail Order email: orders@keypublishing.com
Website: www.keypublishing.com/shop

PUBLISHING
Group CEO: Adrian Cox
Publisher, Books and Bookazines: Jonathan Jackson
Published by
Key Publishing Ltd, PO Box 100, Stamford, Lincs, PE9 1XQ
Tel: 01780 755131
Website: www.keypublishing.com

PRINTING
Precision Colour Printing Ltd, Haldane, Halesfield 1, Telford, Shropshire. TF7 4QQ

DISTRIBUTION
Seymour Distribution Ltd, 2 Poultry Avenue, London, EC1A 9PU
Enquiries Line: 02074 294000.

CONTENTS

THE ROAD TO WATERLOO

Waterloo may be the single most famous battle in history but it was not an isolated event. For more than 20 years the aristocratic nations of Europe had fought against the Revolutionary and Napoleonic regimes in France.

MAIN PICTURE: Napoleon never fully recovered from his abortive invasion of Russia. His *Grande Armée*, some 685,000 strong at the outset of the campaign was reduced to 120,000 by the end. Total deaths are estimated at some 380,000. This is a scene from the retreat through Russia. (Anne S.K. Brown)

Waterloo was the greatest battle of the 19th century and one of the most decisive engagements in military history. It was not like the Somme or El Alamein, or even Blenheim or Salamanca, for these battles brought no conclusion to the conflicts of which they were part. But at Waterloo, in the course of a single day, the Napoleonic Wars were brought to a crushing finale.

An entire generation had grown up knowing little more than a state of war. This almost continual conflict began with the upheavals of the French Revolution. The turmoil in France spread far beyond its borders, embracing most of Europe, even reaching as far afield as the pestilential shores of the Caribbean, the barren steppes of Holy Russia, the bejewelled cities of India and the stormy seas of the Cape.

The wars, which took their name from the son of a minor Corsican aristocrat who crowned himself Emperor of the French, involved more than 30 countries, saw dynasties destroyed and the map of Europe redrawn. Fighting and disease resulted in the deaths of more than 2,500,000 combatants and countless civilians, possibly as many as 7,000,000 in total. It ended in 1815 in a few square miles of muddy Belgian fields.

Most of Europe had turned against France during the bloody days of the Revolution but repeated defeats at the hands of Napoleon Bonaparte had compelled the great powers of Austria, Russia and Prussia to accept peace on French terms. By 1807 Napoleon dominated Europe. He installed his relatives or his Marshals on the thrones of Holland, Westphalia, Naples and Sweden. Much of present-day Belgium and

FAR LEFT: **This painting by Horace Vernet depicts Napoleon on the island of Elba, to where he had been transferred in 1814, awaiting the imminent arrival of *L'Inconstant*, on which he would sail from Porto Ferrajo on 26 February 1815.**

TOP RIGHT: **Fought on 7 September 1812, the Battle of Borodino was a bid by the Russians to stop Napoleon's *Grande Armée* reaching Moscow. With around 70,000 casualties suffered in the fighting, it was the single deadliest day of the Napoleonic Wars.** (Anne S.K. Brown Military Collection, Brown University Library)

northern Italy had been absorbed by France and most of the German states not under direct Napoleonic rule had become satellite states.

Only Great Britain and Portugal, of the principal European nations, remained defiantly at war with France. However, the blockade of most of Europe by the ships of the Royal Navy created severe problems for many of those countries allied to France.

Rumblings of discontent were loudest in St Petersburg and those noises could be heard in Paris.

Fearing yet another coalition of countries led by Russia against France, Napoleon sought to pre-empt any such a combination by attacking first. He assembled the largest army the world had ever seen – an astonishing force of around 680,000 men – and marched into Russia in June 1812.

Tsar Alexander I, after delaying Napoleon in one gruelling battle at Borodino, withdrew deep into Russia, even abandoning Moscow to the invaders. Napoleon entered Moscow, not in triumph, but in silence.

Napoleon came, saw and conquered, but he could not stay. In the heart of Russia, with his lines of communication stretching for hundreds of miles and winter approaching, he could not sustain his army. He had no choice but to abandon his grand expedition and retreat.

In appalling conditions the so-called Grand Army suffered shocking losses, perpetually harassed by the Russians. Only 120,000 men survived the campaign, of whom just 35,000 were Frenchmen. Napoleon had lost his army.

ABOVE: **The Duke of Wellington, commander of the Allied forces in the Waterloo campaign.** (Anne S.K. Brown Military Collection)

RIGHT: **Napoleon on campaign in 1813 sharing a drink with one of his Old Guard.** (Anne S.K. Brown Military Collection)

BELOW: **Napoleon's first abdication resulted from the refusal of his senior officers to fight any longer, led by Marshal Ney.** (Anne S.K. Brown Military Collection)

Realising that an unprecedented opportunity presented itself, Austria and Prussia joined Russia and together they overwhelmed the few troops that Napoleon could muster. Gradually Napoleon was driven back into France until, towards the end of March 1814, the combined Allied armies were just 120 miles from Paris.

Similar events were taking place in the south of France. In 1807 French forces had invaded Portugal and the following year attempted to seize control of Spain. Aided by a small British army, the Portuguese and the Spaniards had fought an almost continuous guerrilla war since that time. For much of the war in the Iberian Peninsula the British army was led by Sir Arthur Wellesley. In victory after victory, Wellesley drove the French out of Portugal and then Spain.

In early 1814 Wellesley, who had by this time had been granted the title of Marquis of Wellington, crossed the Pyrenees and advanced deep into southern France. With enemy forces closing in from all sides Napoleon's marshals refused to obey his orders. It was Marshal Ney, the man Napoleon had dubbed 'the bravest of the brave', who confronted the Emperor. 'The army will not march,' Ney told Napoleon, who was trying to halt the Allied armies before they reached Paris. 'The army will obey me,' insisted Napoleon. 'The army will obey its generals,' replied Ney.

Napoleon had no choice but to accept that the game was up. He offered to abdicate in favour of his three-year-old son, but the Allies would not accept Napoleonic rule by proxy. On 6 April 1814, he renounced the thrones of France and Italy. A week later he agreed to the Treaty of Fontainebleau, in which Bonaparte was awarded the sovereignty of the small Mediterranean island of Elba, with revenue of £2,000,000, to be provided by the French treasury.

The Congress of Vienna

After more than 20 years of warfare, peace returned to Europe, and a corpulent Bourbon prince was restored to the French throne as Louis XVIII. The clock, though, could not be turned back. The upheavals of the previous two decades had changed the face of Europe and many issues had to be resolved. These would be thrashed out at the Congress of Vienna, which began at the end of September 1814.

Considered the most extravagant diplomatic gathering ever witnessed, its objective was to revise the political map of Europe. This included establishing the boundaries of France, the Netherlands, the minor German states, the Italian states and the Duchy of Warsaw. Britain's representative at the Congress was Lord Castlereagh, the Foreign Secretary, being replaced in February 1815 by Wellington who, as a reward for his brilliant performance in what became known as the Peninsular War, had been made a Duke and Field Marshal.

In France, although most welcomed peace, many were unhappy at the return of the monarchy. The French Revolution, with its ideals of liberty, equality and fraternity, elements of which to some degree Napoleon had tried to uphold, had, it seemed, been in vain. The aristocrats were back.

There was also huge dissatisfaction amongst those who had served under Napoleon. The French army was reduced to a peace-footing and thousands of officers and men found themselves dismissed from the service or on half-pay. Even the men of the magnificent Imperial Guard had seen their old titles abolished and their pay reduced.

On the island of Elba, Napoleon was equally dissatisfied. He had not received any of the promised funds from France and the money he had taken with him to Elba was running out. There were rumours that Castlereagh and the French Foreign Minister Talleyrand were planning to deport Napoleon to an even more remote island, possibly in the middle of some distant ocean. He was also well aware of the unrest in France.

LEFT: **The Congress of Vienna was a gathering of senior statesmen from across Europe with the object of creating stability in Europe after two decades of warfare.** (Anne S.K. Brown Military Collection)

Unhappy with his treatment, concerned about his future, and trusting in the huge popularity he once enjoyed in France, Napoleon took the biggest gamble of his life. He decided to escape from Elba and once again seize the throne of France.

Route Napoléon

The story of Napoleon's journey to Paris is a remarkable one. With just the 1,050 men who had been allowed to follow him into exile, Napoleon slipped away from Porto Ferrajo on 26 February 1815 on the brig *L'Inconstant*. Avoiding the Royal Navy patrolling the Mediterranean, Napoleon's little band landed on the south coast of France between Cannes and Antibes.

Despite terrible weather, it took Napoleon's party just six days to reach Grenoble; their route is today proudly marked by monuments. All along the route he took Napoleon was cheered by the people. 'Down with the priests! Down with the nobles! Death to the Royalists! Bourbons to the scaffold!'

At Laffrey, near Grenoble, the narrow defile was blocked by the French 5th Regiment of the Line drawn up in battle order. The opposing forces levelled their muskets. But Napoleon stepped forward. He threw open his coat and offered his breast to the Bourbon troops. 'If any of you will shoot your Emperor,' he declared, 'shoot him now'.

The campaign might have ended at that moment if just one man had pressed his trigger. But Bonaparte's grand gesture had the desired effect, and the men threw down their muskets and flocked around him. When the now much larger band reached Grenoble the peasants battered down the gates; inside stood the garrison, muskets loaded. This was another key moment.

The order to fire rang out, but not a single musket was discharged. When they saw their Emperor the soldiers rushed to embrace him. 'Before Grenoble I was an adventurer,' he later declared. 'At Grenoble I was a reigning prince.'

Marshal Ney, who had led his fellow officers in opposing Napoleon in 1814, and who still held a command under Louis, was sent to capture the erstwhile adventurer. Though he had promised to bring Napoleon to Paris in a cage, he, too, could not resist Napoleon's magnetism. He also joined Napoleon's growing band with his 6,000 men.

There was no mistaking the mood of the people and Louis left Paris with his court at dead of night on 19 March, making for Brussels. Twenty-one hours later Napoleon entered Paris.

Enemy of the World

For all the public acclaim, Napoleon knew that his people did not want to be embroiled in another war. He also knew that Europe was weary of fighting. All he sought, therefore, was to be recognised by the other nations as the *de facto* ruler of France. If the likes of Britain, Austria and Russia would

FROM EXILE TO FRANCE

The brig *L'Inconstant*, ferrying Napoleon to France, crosses the path of the brig *Zéphir* during the journey. *L'Inconstant* flies the tricolour of the Empire, while *Zéphir* flies the white ensign of the French Monarchy. Soldiers of the Imperial Guard are depicted crouching on deck while Napoleon stands fore of the main mast. This painting was ordered by Napoleon himself, with Captain Taillade (of *L'Inconstant*) instructed to provide the artist, Ambroise-Louis Garneray, with all the information and assistance required for its completion.

(Musée National de la Marine)

BOTTOM LEFT: **The scene at Porto Ferrajo during Napoleon's departure in February 1815.** (Musée Naval et Napoléonien du Cap d'Antibes)

NEAR LEFT: ***Maréchal d'Empire* Michel Ney was called 'the bravest of the brave' by Napoleon after he held the French rearguard together during the retreat from Russia. He was also rewarded by Napoleon with the title of Prince de la Moskowa.**

NEAR RIGHT: **Napoleon landed in the Bay of Golfe-Juan, near Antibes, on 1 March 1815.** (Anne S.K. Brown Military Collection.)

FAR RIGHT: **Napoleon's journey from Golfe-Juan to Paris is famous as the Route Napoléon and is still marked as such to this day. It is now a 325-kilometre section of the Route Nationale 85. This picture shows a gilded eagle marker at the southern entry to the town of Gap, the capital of the Hautes-Alpes department.** (Courtesy of Fr. Latreille)

let him sit peaceably on the throne of France there need be no further bloodshed. However, all his peace efforts were ignored. Just five days after reinstalling himself in the Tuileries (a royal and imperial palace in Paris) the great powers of Europe formed the Seventh Coalition, not against France as the previous coalitions had, but against Napoleon himself, whom was described as the 'disturber of the tranquillity of the world'.

Russia, Prussia and Austria agreed to put together a combined force of more than 700,000 men to rid Europe of Bonaparte once and for all. Britain could not provide a large military force but instead provided subsidies, to the tune of £5,000,000, plus another £2,000,000 as an indemnity for not providing her quota of men.

Within a week of reaching this agreement the Allies produced a plan to crush Napoleon. Three armies – the Austrian, 344,000 men under Prince Schwarzenberg; 250,000 British and Prussians under the Duke of Wellington and Field-Marshal Blücher; and a minimum of 200,000 Russians – would march by converging routes on Paris. The assembly of such forces could not be achieved immediately which meant that Napoleon had at least a little time to prepare for the coming onslaught.

Conscription was re-introduced in France in late April but it would be months before these new troops could be trained and equipped. What he would have to fight the Allied armies with would be the old soldiers of 1814. At the most, including all the Bourbon army and those that had been pushed into retirement, France would be able to muster 300,000 experienced soldiers, less than half those of the Allies.

Knowing that he would have to fight, Napoleon then had to decide whether to wait around Paris while his army grew in strength, hoping that the Allies would be sluggish in their mobilisation, or should he strike at the enemy forces already gathering in Belgium close to the French border? If indeed he could attack into Belgium and achieve a stunning victory its impact might induce the former French-controlled parts of the Netherlands to abandon the coalition and rally to the Tricolour. Many in the Netherlands army had once fought under the Imperial Eagle and might do so again. Such a victory might also cause dissent and division in the ranks of the Allies.

In particular Napoleon cast his eyes towards the Anglo-Netherlands army under the command of the Duke of Wellington that was assembling around Brussels. Wellington, undefeated in all his operations against the French, was regarded as the greatest of the Allied generals. Napoleon had never crossed swords with Wellington. Now might be the time to show the world just who was the most brilliant commander. The defeat of Wellington would send shock waves throughout Europe. If Napoleon was to hold onto his throne, sooner or later, he had to beat the Duke of Wellington and sooner would be better.

BELOW: **A view of the historic town of Sisteron on the banks of the River Durance. During the French Revolution, the town had remained Royalist. Consequently when Napoleon arrived there on his march north from Golfe-Juan in 1815, the people of Sisteron ignored him but let him through.** (www.shutterstock.com; Don Simon)

A Mixed Command

On 4 April 1815, Wellington arrived in Belgium to take up his new command. What he found cannot have been very inspiring. His army included the Dutch and Belgium forces of the newly-created Kingdom of the United Netherlands and the various regiments of the Hanoverian militia. He had comparatively few British soldiers.

Following Napoleon's abdication in 1814, the British army had been quickly scaled back. Of those troops that remained under arms a large contingent of some of the best regiments had been sent to North America to bolster the troops in Canada fighting the USA. This all meant that Britain could only muster 25,500 men to face Napoleon. However, the fighting in North America officially ended in February 1815 which meant

that the contingent in Canada would be free to join Wellington – if Bonaparte did not attack first.

In addition to the British troops, Wellington commanded some 6,000 men of the King's German Legion. The KGL had been formed in Britain when Napoleon had overrun King George's Electorate of Hanover in 1803 and a large proportion of its battalions and squadrons had served under Wellington in the Peninsular War. The militia of the regained electorate numbered 15,000 and the United Netherlands army under the command of the Prince of Orange amounted to 29,500 men. The Duke of Brunswick, brother-in-law of the Prince Regent of Britain, added a further 6,700 men and the German Duchy of Nassau contributed another 7,300 troops. This made a combined total of just under 90,000 men, later rising to 107,000.

Wellington Versus Napoleon

This force was not the only one in Belgium facing the French, for on the border with the German states was Blücher's Prussian army of 128,000 men. This made a combined Allied force of more than 200,000 men and according to a Member of Parliament, Thomas Creevey, when he asked Wellington's assessment of the situation, the Duke reputedly remarked, 'By God! I think Blücher and I can do the business'.

Wellington stated that there was simply no need for all the coalition troops to be mobilised before invading France. He calculated that Napoleon would be unable to raise a field force greater than around 150,000 men and therefore the Allied powers should begin operations 'when we shall have 450,000 men', including Russians and Prussians. With such a force Napoleon would be easily crushed.

Wellington's assessment was surprisingly accurate. Such was the energy and enthusiasm of the French people that by 10 June, France had a staggering 504,000 men under arms. Most of these troops, though, were guarding France's southern and western borders or were needed to suppress any uprisings by Royalist supporters. This left Napoleon's striking force of the *l'Armée du Nord* with just 123,000 men and 358 cannon. Nevertheless, Napoleon was going to attack before he was attacked.

The scene was, therefore, set. Napoleon would finally meet Wellington on the battlefield. It was going to be the greatest battle the world had seen.

ABOVE: Napoleon arrived in Paris the day after King Louis had departed. It would be little more than 100 days later that Bonaparte himself would be compelled to leave the French capital after his final resignation. (Anne S.K. Brown Military Collection)

LEFT: A statue of Napoleon at the village of Laffrey, south of Grenoble. Unveiled in 1930, in a spot now known as Prairie de la Rencontre (roughly translated as 'meeting meadow'), the statue marks the spot where Napoleon went forward to meet soldiers sent to detain him. (Emmanuel Frémiet)

FAR LEFT: Unlike the residents of Sisteron, the citizens of Grenoble welcomed Napoleon. (Anne S.K. Brown Military Collection)

NEAR LEFT: A plaque which commemorates Napoleon's entry into Grenoble. (© Guillaume Piolle/ CC-BY-3.0)

COUNTDOWN TO VICTORY

A TIMELINE OF THE BATTLE OF WATERLOO

A view of the battlefield at Waterloo from Wellington's perspective. (Anne S.K. Brown Military Collection, Brown University Library)

26 February
Napoleon sails from Elba with his personal escort of around 600 men.

1 March
Napoleon and his escort land near Antibes on the coast of France and start to march upon Paris.

5 March
The 5th Infantry Regiment, sent to stop Napoleon, deserts to his cause.

13 March
At the Congress of Vienna, the Great Powers of Europe (Austria, Great Britain, Prussia and Russia) and their allies sign a declaration, 'that Napoleon Bonaparte has placed himself without the pale of civil and social relations; and that, as an enemy and disturber of the tranquillity of the world, he has rendered himself liable to public vengeance.'

14 March
Marshal Ney, sent to capture Napoleon and at the same time promising King Louis that he will bring Bonaparte back to Paris in an iron cage, joins the former emperor with 6,000 men.

19 March
Louis XVIII abandons Paris for Brussels.

20 March
Napoleon enters Paris unopposed. The Seventh Coalition, consisting of the United Kingdom, Prussia, Austria, Russia, Hanover, Nassau, Brunswick, United Netherlands, Sweden, Spain, Portugal, Sardinia, Sicily, Tuscany and Switzerland, is formed. The main powers each pledge to put 150,000 soldiers in the field to defeat Napoleon.

28 March
Wellington is appointed Commander-in-Chief of all British land forces.

5 April
Wellington arrives in Brussels to take control of the combined British, Hanoverian, United Netherlands, Brunswick and Nassau troops. Russian armies begin their march southwards.

8 April
Napoleon orders a general mobilization, but refrains from conscription.

21 April
Field Marshal Blücher arrives at Liège where the Prussian Army is forming.

12 June
Napoleon leaves Paris for the Belgian border.

14 June
The various Corps of *l'Armée du Nord* assemble on the Franco-Belgian border. Napoleon issues his orders for the invasion of Belgium. The Prussians prepare to invade France.

15 June

03.30 Leading elements of the French Army cross the frontier into Belgium.

05.00 Prussian outposts south of the River Sambre come under attack and withdraw to Charleroi.

08.00 French troops attack the Charleroi bridge over the Sambre.

11.00 Napoleon arrives at Charleroi and the Imperial Guard take the bridge at bayonet point.

15.00 A Prussian messenger arrives at Brussels to inform Wellington that the French have invaded. Wellington replies that he will concentrate his forces at Quatre Bras.

15.30 Marshal Ney arrives at the front and is given command of the left wing of the army. He is told to advance up the Charleroi to Brussels highway. Grouchy is told to lead the right wing to Sombreffe.

16.00 Blücher arrives at Sombreffe where his army is concentrating. He decides to make a stand at nearby Ligny.

17.45 Cavalry of the French left wing encounter the 2nd Netherlands Division ahead of Quatre Bras.

18.00 Wellington issues his army's marching orders.

21.45 Ney receives word that Quatre Bras is only lightly held by the Allies and he rides there to see the situation for himself.

16 June

00.00-01.00 Wellington receives information that the French are in front of Quatre Bras. He changes his orders, concentrating his forces at Quatre Bras.

05.00 Skirmishes begin at Quatre Bras.

08.00 Napoleon writes to Ney telling him to march on Brussels by a 'quick and sudden movement'. He also tells Grouchy to attack the Prussians if they are found in strength at Sombreffe.

10.00 Wellington arrives at Quatre Bras to assess the situation.

11.00 Napoleon arrives at Fleurus to examine the Prussian positions at Ligny. Blücher intends to make a stand so Napoleon decides to attack him.

13.00 Wellington rides to meet Blücher. Wellington promises Blücher that he will send part of his army to support the Prussians 'providing I am not attacked myself'.

14.00 The Battle of Quatre Bras begins with an attack by Reille's Corps against the Prince of Orange's force holding the crossroads. Napoleon sends a message to Ney informing him that he intends to attack the Prussians at Ligny and ordering the Marshal to attack whatever force of the enemy is directly opposed to him and then having driven it aside to march upon the flank and rear of the Prussians at Ligny.

14.30 Napoleon opens the Battle of Ligny.

15.00 Wellington returns to Quatre Bras. His troops arrive gradually and the French attack is held.

16.00 Ney receives Napoleon's 14.00 hours order and the Marshal decides to send his reserve corps, that of d'Erlon, to attack the crossroads.

16.30 Napoleon sends another message to Ney telling him to 'to manoeuvre immediately in such a manner as to envelop the enemy's right and fall upon his rear'. Shortly afterwards Napoleon receives a message from Ney indicating that he is fully engaged at Quatre Bras. Realising that Ney will not be able to fulfil his earlier order he sends a note to the Marshal to send I Corps to attack the Prussians. The messenger delivers his message directly to I Corps while d'Erlon is reconnoitring Quatre Bras. I Corps changes direction and heads for Ligny.

17.30 The Prussians counter-attack against the French left wing.

18.30 Now powerfully reinforced, Wellington counter-attacks against Ney.

19.00 D'Erlon's corps is seen approaching Napoleon's flank.

19.30 D'Erlon receives a message from Ney ordering him back to Quatre Bras and I Corps turns back to the west.

20.00 Napoleon orders the Imperial Guard, supported by Milhaud's cuirassiers, to attack the Prussian centre.

20.30 The Prussian centre collapses. Blücher covers the retreat with a large force of cavalry. His horse is killed and Blücher is trapped underneath.

21.00 Darkness brings an end to the fighting at Quatre Bras and Ligny.

The Battle of Borodino was a bid by the Russians to stop Napoleon's Grande Armée reaching Moscow. (Anne S.K. Brown Military Collection, Brown University Library)

17 June

06.00 Blücher arrives at Wavre. At first light the Prussian I and II Corps move off to join the rest of the army marching upon Wavre.

07.00 Napoleon is informed that large numbers of Prussians are retreating down the road to Namur, away from Wellington.

07.30 Wellington learns of the Prussian defeat at Ligny and their subsequent retreat. He resolves to withdraw to Mont St Jean and informs the Prussians that if they can support him with one corps he will stand there and give battle.

09.00 Wellington drafts his orders for the withdrawal.

10.00 The Anglo-Allied wounded and the transport wagons begin the withdrawal along the Brussels road.

11.00 Napoleon instructs Grouchy to 'reconnoitre in the direction of Namur, and to pursue the enemy'. He then sets off towards Quatre Bras.

12.00 Wellington's main force begins its withdrawal from Quatre Bras.

13.00 Napoleon reaches Ney's positions and orders him to attack Quatre Bras immediately.

14.00 Ney launches his attack upon Quatre Bras only to find that the Anglo-Allied infantry has gone and that their retreat is being covered by cavalry and horse artillery. The opposing cavalry clash at Genappes. Wellington receives a message from Blücher stating that as Wellington intends to give battle at Mont St Jean IV Corps will attack the French right flank, followed by the rest of the Prussian corps.

18.00 The Anglo-Allied army takes up its positions around Mont St Jean to the north of Waterloo. The French are close behind but are stopped by a volley from the British artillery. Napoleon realises that Wellington is standing to give battle. Bülow's IV Corps reaches the outskirts of Wavre.

18 June

04.00 Napoleon's headquarters receives a despatch from Grouchy stating that the Prussians have split into two columns, one of which is possibly going to join Wellington.

06.00 Wellington leaves Waterloo for Mont St Jean while Bülow's Corps begins its move through Wavre heading for Mont St Jean. The French advance towards La Belle Alliance.

07.00-08.00 Wellington inspects his troops' dispositions and decides to reinforce the Guards at Hougoumont with 1st Battalion 2nd Nassau Regiment. Napoleon and his officers breakfast at Le Caillou. Bülow's Corps experiences delays passing through Wavre.

08.30-09.30 The Anglo-Allied army deploys into its final positions. The leading units of Bülow's Corps finally emerge from Wavre.

09.30-10.00 The Nassau battalion arrives at Hougoumont. Napoleon rides back to near Rossomme Farm, while Blücher sends a message to Wellington telling him that he is marching west to attack the French. At 10.00 Napoleon writes to Grouchy telling him that he is going to attack Wellington and instructing Grouchy to direct his movements on Wavre 'so as to come nearer to us'.

10.00-11.00 1/2 Nassau takes over the defence of the Hougoumont buildings, garden, orchard and wood while the Light Companies of the 2nd (Coldstream) and 3rd Guards move to the kitchen area west of the buildings. Wellington receives a message from the 10th Hussars that a Prussian patrol has confirmed that Bülow is on his way and despatches the 7th Hussars to reconnoitre towards the east. Napoleon receives a message from Grouchy informing him that all his reports confirm that the Prussians are retiring on Brussels or 'to give battle after joining Wellington'. Napoleon then dictates his orders for the attack to capture the village of Mont St Jean.

11.00-12.00 The Anglo-Allied army's deployment is completed. Napoleon rides up to La Belle Alliance and reviews his troops as they take up their positions for the attack. He then changes his orders with the attack now starting with a diversionary attack by Reille on Hougoumont. At 11.20 hours Reille's guns open fire to announce the start of the battle. The gunfire is heard by the Prussians, the leading corps of which have reached Chapelle St Robert. Reille's 1st Brigade from Jerome's 6th Division attacks Hougoumont.

12.00-12.30 The Nassauers and Hanoverians are driven out of Hougoumont Wood and orchard. Bull's troop is brought up to fire its howitzers into the wood. The Light Companies of the 2/1st and 3/1st Guards counter-attack into the wood. Napoleon orders the Grand Battery to be increased to 84 guns and dictates its objectives.

12.30-13.15 Bitter fighting continues at Hougoumont. The leading units of the Prussian IV Corps reach Chapelle-Saint-Lambert. They are spotted by Napoleon who sends another message to Grouchy to 'manoeuvre in our direction'. At 13.00 hours the Grand Battery opens fire.

13.15-14.15 Two companies of 2/3rd Guards are sent to support the men holding the Hougoumont Orchard. Napoleon orders Lobau's VI Corps to block the Prussians. The Lüneberg Battalion of Kielmansegge's Hanoverian Brigade is sent to reinforce the garrison of La Haye Sainte but is caught by Kellerman's Cuirassiers and cut to pieces. Three companies of the 95th withdraw from the sandpit in front of La Haye Sainte. The 'Grand Battery' ceases fire and d'Erlon's I Corps starts its advance upon the Allied right-hand positions. The Household and Union brigades charge I Corps. Ziethen's Prussian Corps marches towards Wellington's left flank. Domon's and Subervie's chasseurs

The 28th Regiment at Quatre Bras on 16 June 1815, by Elizabeth Thompson.

The 28th Regiment at Quatre Bras on 16 June 1815, by Elizabeth Thompson.. (Anne S.K. Brown Military Collection, Brown University Library)

and lancers are sent to help Lobau hold back the Prussians.

14.15-15.00 The Household Brigade attacks and scatters Dubois's cuirassiers while the Union Brigade crashes into I Corps. The French infantry is driven back and the Eagles of the French 45th and 105th regiments are taken. The British cavalry continue onto the Grand Battery, putting it temporarily out of action. Napoleon launches a counter-attack with his heavy and light cavalry against the British cavalry, inflicting heavy losses on the British. The attack upon Hougoumont intensifies as Reille's 5th Division is thrown into the fight.

15.00-16.00 Hougoumont's buildings are set on fire. The La Haye Sainte garrison is reinforced by 1st Battalion KGL and one company of the 5th KGL. 1/95th Rifles re-occupy the sandpit. French and Prussian cavalry clash for the first time that day. The Grand Battery is reorganized and begins to bombard the Allied line again. Ney believes that the Anglo-Allied army is beginning to give way and he orders an unsupported cavalry pursuit.

16.00-17.00 The Allied artillery inflicts heavy casualties on the French cavalry as they charge up Mont St Jean. The British infantry in the first and second lines form battalion squares which the French cavalry cannot penetrate. British cavalry is sent against their French counterparts. Attacks continue against Hougoumont and La Haye Sainte, the troops in the latter run low on ammunition. The Prussians advance upon Plancenoit.

17.00-18.00 Ney brings more cavalry forward and orders them to persist with its attacks despite the fact that no squares have been broken. More reinforcements are sent to La Haye Sainte but the farm is attacked by French infantry again. The whole of Bülow's IV Corps engages Lobau's Corps, driving the French back on Plancenoit. Ziethen's Corps reaches Ohain.

18.00-18.30 The fighting at Hougoumont continues but the buildings remain in Allied hands. The troops in La Haye Sainte run out of ammunition and the French finally take it. The Prussians take Plancenoit and Napoleon sends the Young Guard to win it back.

18.30-19.30 The 5th Line Battalion of the KGL attempts to retake La Haye Sainte but is overrun by cuirassiers. The Hanoverian Cumberland Hussars mutiny and ride off down the road to Brussels. The fighting around Plancenoit intensifies as the village changes hands again with the Prussians taking the village only to be driven out by a battalion of the Old Guard. Ziethen's Corps reaches the left flank of the Allied army, thus securing its flank.

19.30-20.30 The 'crisis' of the battle is reached. Napoleon sends the infantry of the Middle Guards and the Old Guard against Wellington's centre. They are met by Adam's and Halkett's brigades head-on and are assailed by the 52nd Foot on their flank. The Imperial Guard is halted and then thrown back. The cry *'La Garde Récule!* spreads through the French ranks and a general retreat begins. The Prussians, in the form of II Corps re-capture Plancenoit.

20.30-22.00 Wellington orders a general advance as the French retreat turns to a rout. He and Blücher meet at La Belle Alliance. The Battle of Waterloo is over.

19 June

06.00 The bulk of Blücher's force pursues Napoleon's force which is retreating towards the French border. Grouchy attacks Thielemann's II Corps at Wavre.

10.00 Thielemann decides to withdraw under heavy pressure from the French.

10.30 Grouchy receives the news of Napoleon's defeat. He calls his senior officers together and informs them of the situation. He then orders a withdrawal to Namur.

20 June

The French and Prussians march all day. Thielemann catches up with Grouchy near Namur. Grouchy extricates his troops and continues his retreat.

21 June

Wellington and Blücher enter France in two columns and march upon Paris.

22 June

Louis XVIII crosses the border back into France. Napoleon abdicates in favour of his son.

'HUMBUGGED, BY GOD'

For two months Wellington waited for Napoleon to attack. Yet when the French finally crossed the Belgian frontier the Duke was caught unawares and the campaign was almost lost before a shot had been fired. Why?

On 25 March 1815, Britain, Austria, Russia and Prussia agreed to place 150,000 men in the field to defeat Napoleon, who had reclaimed the throne of France barely a week before. A grand strategy was devised in which the combined armies of those countries would converge on France and march upon Paris. After putting his name to this agreement, Wellington set out for the Low Countries to take command of the Anglo-Netherlands army, arriving in Brussels – the capital of the recently-created Kingdom of the United Netherlands – on 4 April.

Prior to Wellington's arrival, the Allied army in Belgium had been under the command of William, the Hereditary Prince of Orange. To his credit the Prince had taken measures to defend the Belgian frontier as soon as he had learnt of Napoleon's return from Elba. The Prince had moved his small force (approximately 20,000 men) towards the Franco-Belgian border around the town of Ath. Mons and Tournai were also occupied and work set in hand to strengthen both towns' defences. To the east, the Anglo-Dutch outposts reached as far as Namur where they touched the right wing of General Kleist's Prussian Army of the Lower Rhine. The two Allied commanders had agreed to combine forces if the French should strike into Belgium.

This, then, was the situation in the Low Countries when Wellington assumed command of the Anglo-Netherlands Army. With his usual energy Wellington began to bombard his government with demands for more men and equipment. He also began to plan offensive operations in the knowledge that reinforcements were on their way, while more troops from Prussia, Austria and Bavaria would also soon be on the move to join the forces on the Belgian border.

The plan of operations would see the Anglo-Dutch and Prussian armies spearheading an advance into France backed up by the other Allied armies when they arrived. Wellington was given the role of overall commander of the Allied armies for this operation, which it was hoped would begin in June. This plan, of course, assumed that Napoleon would remain passively waiting for the Allies to crush him with superior numbers. →

MAIN PICTURE: 'The most famous ball in history'. Thus did Wellington biographer Elizabeth Longford describe the Duchess of Richmond's ball, held in Brussels on 15 June 1815.
(All Images Courtesy of Anne S.K. Brown Military Collection, Brown University Library unless othrwise stated)

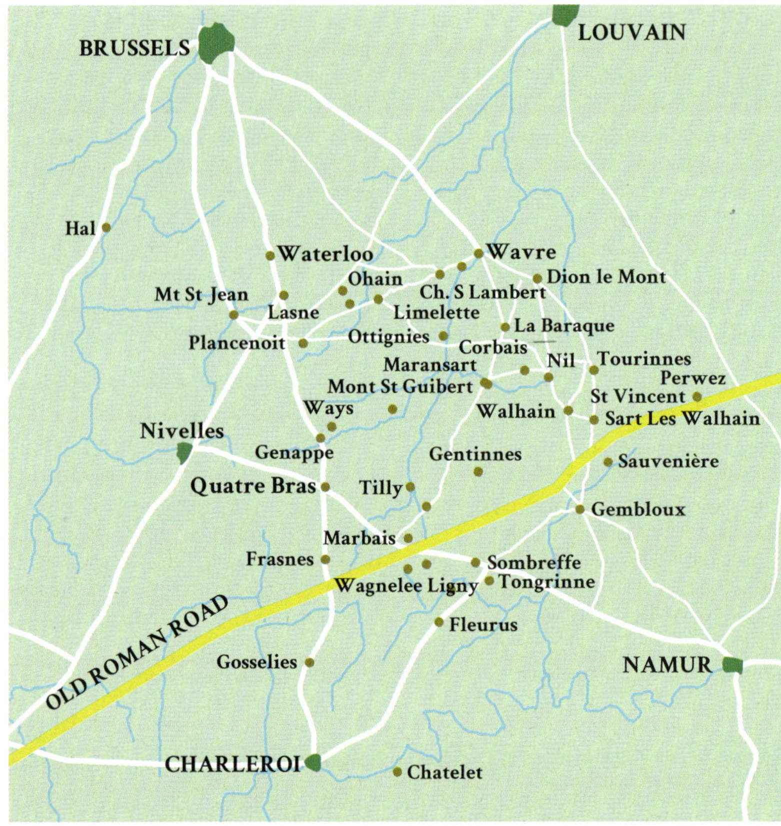

TOP LEFT: Chasseurs à Cheval of the Imperial Guard on the march.

TOP RIGHT: Map showing the principal locations relating to the Battle of Waterloo.

RIGHT: General Wilhelm von Dörnberg, though Prussian, was a member of the Brunswick Legion that served with the British Army. He was Wellington's eyes and ears on the Belgian/French border. He commanded the British 3rd Brigade at Quatre Bras and Waterloo.

BOTTOM LEFT (OPPOSITE PAGE): British infantry on the march in 1815. This appears to be a fusilier regiment, possibly the 23rd Royal Welch Fusiliers.

This, though, was not Napoleon's way. Wellington and the Prussian commander, Field Marshal Gebhard von Blücher, were therefore anxious to take the offensive in May, but there was little prospect that the Austrians would have fully mobilized by then or that the Russians would have covered the vast distance from their motherland by that time. So for two months Wellington and Blücher would have to stand on the defensive and hope that Napoleon would not attack before they could start their own operations.

Anxious Wait

Appreciating the potentially dangerous position he was in, Wellington devoted considerable attention to the defence of the Belgian frontier and arranged for the strengthening of the frontier fortresses. Having put that measure in hand, he had to consider the positioning of his troops.

The Duke could not simply place his divisions in the best position to fight a defensive battle in conjunction with the Prussians. He had first to cover the British Army's communications with the ports of Ostend and Antwerp. Second, he had to protect the town of Ghent where the erstwhile King of France and his government-in-exile had taken up temporary residence.[1] Third, he had to defend the new capital of the United Netherlands. Fourth, he had to safeguard the lines of retreat of the Dutch and Hanoverian armies. In addition to these considerations, Wellington could not hope to stop the French Army without the assistance of the Prussians, and the positions that his army would eventually adopt would, at least in part, reflect this.

Wellington detailed his views to the Prussian Army's Chief of Staff, General August Gneisenau, in a letter dated 5 April 1815. He stated that he believed that Napoleon would advance into Belgium between the Scheldt and the Sambre rivers so as to strike at the British Army's communications with the Channel ports. If this happened, the Prussian and Anglo-Netherlands armies should withdraw together north-east towards Liège and Maastricht. This meant that the British line back to the coast would be sacrificed, but equally it meant that the two Allied armies would remain together and would have fallen back towards the oncoming Austrian and Russian armies.[2]

This satisfied Gneisenau as it kept open the Prussian line of retreat eastwards, and, in a similar gesture, Gneisenau concentrated his troops as far west, and as close to Wellington's troops, as he could, around Charleroi.

Wellington spread his forces in a wide convex arc from Courtrai, through Tournai and Mons, to Quatre Bras. This wide dispersal was designed to ensure that any French penetration across the border was immediately detected, and to ease the army's billeting and supply problems. It meant, however, that it would take many hours of marching for the army to assemble. Wellington, consequently, issued detailed instructions to his corps commanders instructing them precisely where to assemble and which points to occupy in the event of a French attack.

An Open Border

If Napoleon struck towards the west of Brussels and the Channel ports, the British infantry divisions would concentrate around Oudenarde, Enghien, Soignies, Grammont and Ath, with the cavalry covering the army's right flank. The Netherlands' divisions would pull back to form the left flank of the army, around Soignies and Nivelle. If the attack was delivered through the much wider corridor between the Sambre and the Scheldt, the whole Anglo-Netherlands force would assemble immediately south of Brussels at Hal, Enghien, Soignies, and Braine le Comte.

The Belgian frontier with France is naturally open to invasion along most of its length except to the east of Namur where the difficult forested country of the Ardennes is found. There were four principal routes that ran over this border to Brussels and Wellington believed that if Napoleon attacked it would be along the road that ran from Paris, through Valenciennes, Maubeuge, and Mons and on to Brussels. He dismissed the Paris, Charleroi, Quatre Bras, Waterloo, Brussels road because if Napoleon adopted that route he would be placing himself right in the middle of the Prussian and Anglo-Netherlands armies – but, as it would transpire, that is exactly what Napoleon planned to do.

Throughout May Wellington received a mass of information indicating the build up of enemy forces to the south of the Belgian border. Though much of this intelligence was intentional misinformation on the part of the French, it did prompt Wellington to move his own forces somewhat closer together. But as Wellington complained to the Prince of Orange, 'In the situation in which we are placed at present, neither at war nor at peace, unable on that account to patrol up to the enemy and ascertain his position by view, it is difficult, if not impossible, to combine an operation.' In fact there was little more that Wellington could do to improve his defensive arrangements. All he could hope was that his Allies would arrive before Napoleon could strike.[3]

In the first week of June, very specific information was received from a French deserter indicating that French troops were being moved up to the border on wagons. On the 11th of the month Wellington received a report which stated that a French artillery park of 250 guns had been assembled at Valenciennes and that French infantry had collected around Maubeuge.

At this point Wellington must have wondered exactly what Napoleon was planning as these movements did not appear to conform with his reading of the situation. Even more alarming was that on the morning of the 14th, he learned that the assembled French army, having been provided with eight days' rations, was heading towards Beaumont.

This meant that the French were moving eastwards and away from the invasion route Wellington had expected. Yet he was so convinced that Napoleon would attack to the west, he made no move to counter this sudden shift. A few hours later, at 04.30 hours on 15 June 1815, the outposts of the Prussian I Corps were attacked. The Waterloo campaign had begun.

Opening Moves

The commander of the Prussian I Corps, *Generalleutnant* Graf von Zieten, immediately sent a courier to Brussels with news of the French attack across the Sambre. Von Zieten asked Wellington if he would concentrate his forces at Nivelles where they could more readily support the Prussian right wing.

This despatch reached Wellington at approximately 09.00 hours, but in the absence of any confirmatory reports from his own outposts Wellington preferred to wait until he was certain about exactly what was happening. Even after the Prince of Orange had ridden to Brussels (arriving there at around 15.00 hours) to inform Wellington that the Prussians had been attacked, Wellington 'did not deem it expedient to make any alteration in his position, until the enemy should further develop his mode of attack'.[4]

TOP RIGHT: Grenadiers à Cheval of Napoleon's Imperial Guard on the march.

FAR LEFT: The Duke of Brunswick's small force formed part of Wellington's army in the Waterloo campaign. His men wore black uniforms with a death's head skull and crossbones on their shakos in memory of the Duke's father, who was killed by the French in 1806 at the battle of Jena-Auerstedt.

ABOVE LEFT: An infantryman of the Netherlands Army. The Royal Netherlands Army was formed on 9 January 1814, following the uprising against Napoleonic rule in 1813.

BOTH ABOVE: Two of a remarkable set of photographs of 15 French veterans from the Napoleonic Wars wearing their original uniforms. Left is a soldier called Maire of the 7th Hussars. The other is a man named Mauban of the 8th Dragoon Regiment of 1815.

BELOW LEFT: The Prince of Orange was the heir apparent to the Kingdom of the Netherlands. He had previous military experience as he had served as an aide-de-camp to Wellington in the Iberian Peninsula. He was reputedly very courageous and was well-liked in the British Army.

FAR RIGHT: An encampment of Highland troops, in this instance what would appear to be the 42nd Foot.

About 30 minutes later a despatch arrived from Blücher at Namur confirming the direction of the French advance. Yet still Wellington would not commit himself. All he would do, he told Major General Baron von Müffling, the Prussian liaison officer at Wellington's headquarters, was 'wait for my advices from Mons before I fix my rendezvous [of the army]. Nevertheless, as the breaking up from cantonments is certain, and only the point of assembly doubtful, I shall order all to be in readiness.'

The orders for the army to break camp and be prepared to move were issued between 18.00 and 19.00 hours – some ten hours after Wellington had received the first Prussian despatch.[5]

The French attack had been developing for almost 12 hours and still Wellington clung to his conviction that Napoleon would advance through Mons, even though there was not one piece of evidence at all to support this theory. The next development occurred sometime between 19.00 hours and 22.00 hours when von Müffling received another communication from Blücher.

'A second report reached me later from Charleroi via Namur,' recalled von Müffling. 'General Blücher informed me in this of his concentration at Sombrel, and desired me to inform him of the concentration [of the British Army] before receiving his accounts from Mons. He promised me instant intelligence on receipt.'

Wellington In Denial

Von Müffling then went back to his quarters where he drew up his report for Blücher but, as Wellington had still not committed himself to any course of action, the places where the Anglo-Netherlands forces would concentrate had to be left blank. He arranged for a courier's carriage to be held in readiness outside the door to his quarters to send off the report as soon as Wellington made up his mind.

The Prussians clearly believed that they were facing the principal French attack, and although Wellington still had not received one scrap of information to counter this view, he refused to accept the fact that Napoleon had placed himself directly in the middle of the British and Prussian armies, where he was likely to be crushed. Of course Napoleon was only likely to be crushed if Wellington and Blücher combined together to fall upon the French, and that is exactly what was not happening.

That night a ball was being held by the Duchess of Richmond in a coach house in Brussels. The duchess's husband, Charles Lennox, commanded a reserve force stationed in Brussels, and all but three of Wellington's senior officers made a point of attending the ball, despite the fact that the enemy were known to have crossed the border just a few miles to the south. Wellington himself was determined to maintain an appearance of calm and normality, so he also went to the ball.

Von Müffling likewise was going to this glamorous social event and as he was getting ready to go out he received a note from Wellington, which read: 'I have a report from General Dörnberg [in command of the 3rd Cavalry Brigade] at Mons that Napoleon has moved on Charleroi with all his force, and that he, General Dörnberg, has nothing in his front. I have therefore sent orders for the concentration of my people on Nivelles and Quatre Bras.'

The orders that Wellington was referring to were timed at '10 o'clock, PM'. Although Wellington had told von Müffling that he was going to concentrate his forces at Nivelles and Quatre Bras, his orders, which still exist, make no mention of Quatre Bras at all. Instead the Anglo-Netherlands divisions

LEFT: **A Grenadier of the British 40th Foot. This regiment formed part of the British 6th Division which, with the 5th Division, constituted Wellington's reserve.**

were told to gather around Enghien and Nivelles. Such a move would have meant that Quatre Bras, a vital crossroads, would have been left completely unguarded.

Disobeying Orders

Already holding Quatre Bras were elements of the 2nd Netherlands Brigade under Prince Bernhard of Saxe-Weimar. Fortunately for Wellington, Jean Victor Baron de Constant Rebecque, the Chief-of-Staff of the Netherlands Army, had ordered General Perponcer, commander of the 2nd Dutch Division, to send Prince Bernhard to occupy the crossroads at Quatre Bras. When the order was received from Wellington for the concentration of the army, Rebecque decided to disregard the Duke's instructions and retain possession of the crossroads. If Rebecque had followed Wellington's orders, Quatre Bras would have been left entirely unguarded. As will be seen, Rebecque unquestionably saved Wellington's reputation with that instruction to General Perponcher.

As he was told to hold his ground, Prince Bernhard asked for more support from the 1st Netherlands Brigade as he had heard gunfire in the direction of Frasnes, which indicated that the French were near. Consequently, a small but significant force was assembled at Quatre Bras which would play a very large part in the events to come over the next few hours.

The Duchess of Richmond's Ball

The Duke of Wellington and Baron von Müffling went off to the ball at around midnight. Now regarded as perhaps the most famous ball in history, it was a grand affair with the aristocratic officers in their silver and gold laced scarlet and blue uniforms dancing with the beautiful women of London and Brussels high society.

Shortly before supper a soldier entered the ballroom. Lieutenant Henry Webster was clearly in a hurry, with important news to impart. He handed a despatch from Rebecque to his commander, the Prince of Orange, who passed it, unopened, to the Duke. Wellington read the despatch and then, not wishing to create alarm, slid the note quietly into his pocket. He then advised the Prince to miss supper and make haste to join his troops.

Following a few whispered instructions to his staff, Wellington sat down to eat. After a few minutes of polite conversation, Wellington announced that it was time for him to go to bed. The party rose and went into the hall. As he was preparing to leave he whispered into the Duke of Richmond's ear, 'Have you a good map in the house?'

Richmond took Wellington into his study next to the ballroom and spread out his map. The message from Rebecque, timed around 22.00 hours, contained the shocking news that the Netherlands forces had been engaged with the French in front of Quatre Bras.

As Wellington looked at the map he must have realised that the enemy was just a march away from Brussels and that if the French pushed on without delay they could be in the new capital of the Netherlands while his own army was still scattered around the countryside. Somehow Napoleon had pushed his way between the two Allied armies. 'Napoleon has humbugged me, by God!' Wellington exclaimed. 'He has gained 24 hours' march on me.'

Richmond asked Wellington what he intended to do. 'I have ordered the army to concentrate at Quatre Bras; but we shall not stop him there, and if so, I must fight him here.' As he spoke, Wellington passed his thumb along the map, just below a small village called ... Waterloo.[6]

LEFT: ***Generalmajor*** **Baron Friedrich Karl Ferdinand Freiherr von Müffling was the Prussian commissioner, or liaison officer, at Wellington's headquarters.**

NOTES:

1. Jac Weller, *Wellington at Waterloo* (Greenhill, London 1992), p.181.
2. John Fortescue, *A History of the British Army*, (Macmillan, London, 1920), vol. X, pp.257-8.
3. John Gurwood [Ed], *The Dispatches of Field Marshal the Duke of Wellington, K.G. during his various campaigns in India, Denmark, Portugal, Spain, the Low Countries, and France* (Murray, London, 1838) vol.12, p.375.
4. Fortescue, *op. cit.*, p.277.
5. C. von Müffling, *History of the Campaign in the Year 1815 etc.*, (T. Egerton, London, 1816) p.xiii.
6. Elizabeth Longford, *Wellington, The Years of the Sword* (Weidenfeld and Nicholson, London, 1969), pp.420-1.

'THE FATE OF FRANCE'

Napoleon called Marshal Ney 'the bravest of the brave' and at the Battle of Quatre Bras he gave Ney the responsibility of holding the Anglo-Netherlands forces in check whilst he attacked the Prussians at Ligny.

MAIN PICTURE: ***The 28th Regiment at Quatre Bras*** **by Elizabeth Thompson. The artist chose to portray the moment at 17.00 hours on 16 June 1815, 'when the gallant 28th braced itself for one massive, final charge of terrifying Polish Lancers and cuirassier veterans led by Marshal Ney'.**

Maréchal Michel Ney epitomised the ideals upon which Napoleon's Imperial Army was built. He had been born in 1769 as the son of a barrel cooper. After a dull, if brief, career as a civil servant, at the age of 18 he enlisted in the French Army. By the time he rode up to Napoleon's headquarters on 15 June 1815, to be given command of the left wing of the army, he had fought on a multitude of battlefields and had risen to a place in the French nobility. Not only was he a Marshal of the Empire, and a Duke, he was also a prince – Prince de la Moskowa. Napoleon had sought to promote on grounds of merit, not birth, declaring that 'there is a marshal's baton in every knapsack'. If any of his men should doubt that, they need look no further than Michel Ney. Once Napoleon had decided to split his army, there was probably no one better to take command of one of its wings.

Ney, though, had history. It had been Ney that had demanded Napoleon's abdication the previous year, informing Napoleon that the army would no longer fight.

Napoleon saw Ney's actions as nothing but betrayal and, since his return from exile, Napoleon had not involved Ney in any of his planning nor had he included his name in any of the despatches he had issued since the start of operations. Ney had only been summoned to join the army as Napoleon left Paris on 12 June and the Corps commanders whom Ney was now given authority over were unaware of his presence in the field. The consequences of this will be seen shortly.

FAR LEFT: The Prince of Orange overlooking the battlefield at Quatre Bras.

NEAR LEFT: The majority of the Prussian regiments were *Landwehr*, which were conscripted troops. All males between the ages of 18 and 45 not serving with the regular army were liable for service in the *Landwehr*.

(All Images Courtesy of Anne S.K. Brown Military Collection, Brown University Library unless otherwise stated)

The Road To Quatre Bras

According to Napoleon, when he gave Ney command of the left wing he told him to 'move at first light on the 16th beyond Quatre Bras and take up a good position astride the Brussels road, guarding the Nivelles and Namur roads with his left and right wings'. Ney galloped up towards Quatre Bras on the evening of the 15th expecting no opposition.

On the way he came upon the leading units of II Corps which formed part of his new command. This unit had encountered elements of the Prussian army (Steinmetz's 1 Brigade) at Gosselies which were covering Blücher's withdrawal towards Ligny.

The French advance guard attacked the Prussians who withdrew eastwards. The road to Quatre Bras was now open. But Ney wanted to be sure.

He halted II Corps and sent forward the Imperial Guard Light Cavalry Division (which Napoleon had given to Ney to indicate to the Corps commanders that he was operating with the Emperor's consent) to investigate the situation at Quatre Bras. He also sent his leading division of infantry and a large proportion of the 2nd Cavalry Division in the direction which the Prussians had gone because he had heard the sound of cannon fire in that direction.

When the Guard cavalry reached Quatre Bras, its commander, General Lefèbvre-Desnoëttes, found that far from being empty, the crossroads were held by the outposts of the 2nd Netherlands Division and the 2nd Nassau Regiment backed by a battery of Dutch horse artillery. When the Guards probed the Dutch positions they were driven off by the eight guns of the horse artillery.

It was evident that the only way that Ney could take the crossroads was by bringing up infantry and artillery to support the Guard cavalry. It was now nearly dark, however, and such an operation was not feasible. As the Allied force at Quatre Bras was only small, Ney remained confident that he would have enough troops assembled by morning to carry out his instructions. →

ABOVE: **At Quatre Bras the 69th Foot was caught still trying to form square by French cuirassiers, with disastrous results. This image shows the Commanding Officer of the 69th, Colonel Middlebury, escaping from the French.**

All, though, was not quite as satisfactory as it appeared. Ney had no real idea where most of his troops were. His late, and unexpected, appointment to command the left wing meant that he had not been able to liaise properly with General Reille's II Corps and had only written communication with d'Erlon's I Corps.

Ney returned to Napoleon's headquarters at Charleroi, reaching there about midnight. While discussing the situation over supper, Napoleon rebuked Ney for wasting time in chasing after the retreating Prussians just because he heard cannon fire. He should have stuck strictly to his orders. If he had pushed on with his infantry in support of the Guard cavalry he could already be in possession of Quatre Bras. Marshal Grouchy was also having supper that night with Napoleon and Ney. He would remember well Napoleon's words. They would cost France its empire.

RIGHT: **A drummer of the 92nd Regiment, the Gordon Highlanders. The Gordons were in the British centre throughout the Battle of Quatre Bras, repeatedly forming line to fire on advancing French infantry, and squares to repel cavalry.**

Wellington's Reputation

The early hours of 16 June saw Ney trying to organise his new command so that he could push on to Quatre Bras; but already the Anglo-Allied army was bearing down on the crossroads. Napoleon's rapid advance of the 15th had so surprised Wellington that the various divisions of his command were quite unprepared for the move he now expected from them.

It would be many hours before they could reach Quatre Bras in anything like large numbers. Captain Mercer, in command of 'G' Troop, Royal Horse Artillery, has left us an example of the confusion of those first hours of the Waterloo campaign: 'I was immediately sensible of another error – that of having started out without a guide; for the roads became so numerous, intricate, and bad, often resembling only woodmen's tracks, that I was sorely puzzled, spite of the map I carried in my sabretache, to pick out my way. But a graver error still I had now to reproach myself with, and one that might have been attended with fatal consequences. Eager to get on, and delayed by the badness of the roads, I left all my ammunition wagons behind.'[2]

The result of such confusion and the fact that Wellington's force was so widely spread meant that Quatre Bras was still only held by the 7,373 men of the 2nd Netherlands Division under General Hendrik de Perponcher when Wellington arrived there a little before 10.00 hours. These troops had been fully occupied by the French all morning.

Ney had sent reconnaissance patrols towards the crossroads to test the strength of the Allied position, but had not yet committed his troops to an all-out assault. He had been told to occupy the crossroads at first light and was intending to attack Quatre Bras at dawn with all the force he had available. However, General Reille remembered from his battles with Wellington in the Peninsular War how the Duke carefully concealed his men. Reille feared that there were more Allied troops opposite him than there appeared to be and he pleaded with Ney to wait until more battalions had arrived before delivering the attack.

Ney was known to be bold and impetuous but that morning he accepted Reille's advice and the attack was suspended until the rest of II Corps marched up. Wellington's reputation saved the Allies at Quatre Bras, for the longer Ney waited the stronger the forces opposite him became.[3] As the small Dutch and Nassau force would,

GNEISENAU

Generalleutnant August Wilhelm Antonius Graf Neidhardt von Gneisenau was Blücher's Chief of Staff during the Waterloo campaign. Blücher was injured in the closing stages of the Battle of Ligny and was temporarily out of touch with his staff. This left Gneisenau with sole responsibility for deciding in which direction the Prussian army should retreat. He chose to withdraw towards Wavre which meant that the Prussians were still close to Wellington's army. Had Gneisenau retreated eastwards back along his line of communication, the Battle of Waterloo might never have been fought.

in time, be reinforced with the rest of Wellington's army marching up to Quatre Bras, the duke felt confident enough to leave his troops and ride over to the east to see what the Prussians were doing.

The Prussians At Ligny

Wellington met Blücher at Brye just to the north of the village of Ligny beyond which the French army was concentrating. It was apparent that Napoleon was going to attack the Prussians and it was equally clear that the Prussians were going to stand and fight. Blücher's chief of staff, General Gneisenau, asked Wellington to send his troops to support the Prussians, but all that Wellington would commit to was that he would join the Prussians, 'provided I am not attacked myself'. With that Wellington rode back to Quatre Bras to see what was happening there.

In the meantime Ney had received a message from the Emperor. In this Napoleon advised Ney that he was sending him the Cavalry Corps of General Kellerman to join his command and that, 'With these forces, you must beat and destroy all the enemy corps which may present themselves. Blücher was in Namur yesterday and it is not likely that he will have moved troops towards Quatre Bras. So you have to deal only with what comes from Brussels.'[4]

The orders were carried by Napoleon's Imperial ADC, General Count Flahaut, who was instructed to explain to Ney that he should 'move to Quatre Bras, to hold this important point in strength, and [should the situation permit] to support with every man at his disposal the Emperor's offensive against the Prussian army'.[5]

Ney could be in no doubt what was required of him. He issued orders for Reille to take Quatre Bras with D'Erlon being told to concentrate three of his four divisions at Frasnes to form the reserve with the other division being posted at Marbais to the east to maintain contact between Ney's left wing and the Emperor's force at Ligny.

It was at 14.00 hours that Ney launched his attack upon Quatre Bras. His first objective was to take the Bois de Bossu as it would be impossible for him to advance against the crossroads with the wood being occupied by the Allies on his flank. Upon advice from Reille, rather than attack directly through the wood, where the British positions could not be known, II Corps was ordered to take the farm of Pierrepoint on the extreme western side of the wood. If the latter was held in strength by the Allies, as Reille feared, this flanking move would drive them out.

With Reille's men swinging round the side of the Bois de Bossu, and an attack developing on their right front, Perponcher's men fell back towards the crossroads whilst still keeping some troops in possession of the wood.

Around this time, fortunately, the Prince of Orange arrived with 8,000 men and sixteen guns. Ney's task was becoming harder with every passing minute.

Reinforcements Arrive

Wellington also rode back from Ligny a few minutes later accompanied by von Müffling. 'On our return to Quatre Bras we found Marshal Ney fully engaged in the attack, which had begun on the farm of Gemioncourt, occupied by us,' von Müffling wrote in his memoirs. 'The enemy, with their two *corps d'armée*, displayed such great superiority over Perponcher's division, that it was evidently impossible, unless some extraordinary circumstances intervene, to hold Quatre Bras.'[6] →

TOP LEFT: An officer of the French 1st Cuirassier Regiment. The cuirassiers almost tipped the scales of victory in Ney's favour at Quatre Bras.

TOP RIGHT: The 7th Queen's Own Hussars under Sir Edward Kerrison, charging the French at Quatre Bras.

ABOVE RIGHT: The Battle of Ligny as depicted by Theodore Yung.

LEFT: Colonel John Cameron commanded the 92nd at Quatre Bras, where he was killed leading his men in an attack on a house on the Charleroi road which was held by the French.

RIGHT: The Duke of Brunswick was killed at Quatre Bras leading his cavalry in an attempt to drive back French skirmishers who were 'crowding' his men.

Just as the Netherlands Light Cavalry Brigade rode up to Quatre Bras, the French attack increased in ferocity. But now the first battalions of the British infantry divisions were marching up to the crossroads.

Wellington, aware that the French pressure was mounting, decided to do what von Müffling called 'a resolution worthy of a great commander'. When it might be expected that Wellington would withdraw under the weight of the French onslaught, he did the exact opposite – he attacked.

He ordered the Brunswickers and Picton's 5th Division to advance, with the result that the infantry of General Bachelu's 5th Division of Reille's Corps was pushed backwards. Wellington's plan seemed to be working – but then the French 2nd Brigade of Piré's 2nd Cavalry Division (two regiments of Chasseurs and two of Lancers) suddenly struck, as Sergeant James Anton of the 42nd Highlanders recalled:

'A German [KGL] orderly dragoon galloped up exclaiming, "Franchee! Franchee!" and, wheeling about, galloped off. We instantly formed a rallying square; no time for particularity: every man's piece was loaded, and our enemies approaching at full charge; the feet of their horses seemed to tear up the ground. Our skirmishers ... fell beneath their lances, a few escaped death or wounds; our brave Colonel [Sir Robert Macara] fell at this time, pierced through the chin until the point reached his brain. Captain [Archibald] Menzies fell covered in wounds.'[7]

Picton's advance stalled under this onslaught from the French cavalry and on the other side of the crossroads reinforcements had helped Prince Jerome Bonaparte's 6th Division penetrate into the Bois de Bossu. The battle was evenly balanced and both Ney and Wellington knew that the next moves might prove decisive.

However, Ney had received a message from Napoleon (timed at 14.00 hours) stating that the Prussians had collected 'a Corps of troops' near Ligny which the Emperor intended to attack. Ney was told that after he had captured Quatre Bras he should turn in Napoleon's direction 'so as to bring about the envelopment of that body of the enemy's troops', i.e. the Prussian Corps.

As he already had d'Erlon's Corps posted towards Ligny, this instruction did not worry Ney. However, a second message reached Ney a little more than an hour later – and this one must have shocked the Marshal. After informing Ney that battle with the Prussians was in full swing, Marshal Soult, Napoleon's chief-of-staff, wrote: 'His Majesty desires me to tell you that you are to manoeuvre immediately in such a manner as to envelop the enemy's right and fall upon his rear; the army in our front is lost if you act with energy.'

If this was not alarming enough for Ney who was fully engaged with the Anglo-Dutch forces and little able to extract himself without great difficulty, the next words were nothing short of shocking. 'The fate of France is in your hands. Thus do not hesitate even for a moment to carry out the manoeuvre ordered by your Emperor.'[8]

Confusion

What on earth was Ney to do? From a seemingly secondary role he had suddenly been told that the entire campaign, indeed the entire future of his country, rested upon his shoulders. As he saw it, the only way he could carry out Napoleon's instructions was by quickly defeating Wellington so that he could then turn his attention to helping defeat the Prussians. For this he would

BELOW: Blücher's horse was shot when the 72-year-old Prussian leader was leading a charge against the French at the Battle of Ligny. The horse fell on top of him, and Blücher was badly concussed. He was rescued by one of his aides still barely conscious.

need every available man, and that meant calling up d'Erlon's Corps.

Unfortunately Napoleon had a similar idea. After sending Ney the fateful message he realised that what he had asked of Ney might not be possible. After all, he, Napoleon, did not know how many Anglo-Dutch troops were in front of Ney. He decided that he could not take the chance of waiting for Ney, who might never come, and instead ordered d'Erlon to march upon Ligny and take the Prussians in the flank.

Napoleon sent his Imperial Aide de Camp, General le Compte de la Bedoyère, with a message for d'Erlon. This read: 'The enemy is falling headlong into the trap I have laid for him. Proceed immediately with all your forces to the heights of Ligny and fall on Saint Amand. Monsieur le Compte d'Erlon, you are about to save France and cover yourself with glory.'[9] D'Erlon sent a message to Ney informing him that I Corps was marching for Ligny.

Ney, upon receiving d'Erlon's message, was speechless! Ney had been placed in an impossible situation. In what must have been a state of seething anger and stifling frustration he decided to countermand his Emperor's order.

Another messenger set off with yet another message. This messenger did indeed carry the fate of France in his hands. For the message he carried reminded d'Erlon that he was under Ney's command and that he should immediately turn round and march upon Quatre Bras with the utmost urgency.

This message reached d'Erlon just as his leading units marched to within sight of the battle that was raging around Ligny. Napoleon was informed that d'Erlon was close at hand and would soon fall upon the Prussians. A great victory was about to unfold.

Contradiction

Upon receiving Ney's order d'Erlon was faced with the same dilemma that Ney had been presented with. In the end he decided that Ney was his immediate superior and that he must be in terrible trouble if he had called so urgently for his return. So, just as Napoleon expected to see d'Erlon strike at the Prussians, the I Corps' column, seemingly inexplicably, began to march away. The time was around 18.00 hours.

So, within sight of one battlefield, d'Erlon had turned round and marched towards another battlefield. He did not reach Quatre Bras until 20.00 hours. By then it was getting late and, with night creeping in, the fighting around the crossroads died down at about 21.00 hours. Wellington had held the crossroads.

Napoleon defeated the Prussians at Ligny, but it was not the crushing victory he had hoped for. D'Erlon's Corps of 20,000 men would have proven decisive at either battle. Instead I Corps spent all afternoon and evening marching backwards and forwards for nothing.

The fault here lies squarely with Napoleon. He had told Ney to seize Quatre Bras and had placed two corps under him for that task. He could not then take half of that force away from the Marshal and still expect him to accomplish his mission. It was he, not Ney, who had held the fate of France in his hands and it was he who had let it slip through his fingers.

LEFT: **Close to the crossroads at Quatre Bras, on the road to Nivelles, is this monument to the Dutch-Belgian cavalry of the 1815 campaign.** (Courtesy of John Grehan)

LEFT: **A view of Gemioncourt Farm, which is situated to the south of the crossroads at Quatre Bras. The French seized Gemioncourt in their early attacks, but by the end of the battle it was back in Allied hands.** (Courtesy of John Grehan)

LEFT: **The crossroads at Quatre Bras – the 'Four Arms'. Here the Charleroi to Brussels highway is crossed by the Namur to Nivelles road.** (Courtesy of John Grehan)

LEFT: **Napoleon surrounded by his staff surveying the battlefield of Ligny at the windmill of Brye. Painted by Ernest Crofts, 1875.**

NOTES:

1. D. Chandler, *The Campaigns of Napoleon*, (Macmillan, New York, 1966), p.1001.
2. W. H. Fitchett (Ed.), *Waterloo 1815, Captain Mercer's Journal* (Pen & Sword, Barnsley, 2012), p.46.
3. Sir John Fortescue, *The Campaign of Waterloo* (Greenhill, London, 1989), p.91.
4. William Seymour, Eberhard Kaulbach, Jacques Champagne, *Waterloo: Battle of Three Armies* (Book Club Associates, 1979), p.200.
5. Hamilton-Williams, *op. cit.*, pp.195-6.
6. Baron Karl von Müffling, *The Memoirs of Baron Von Müffling*, (Greenhill, London, 1997), pp.237-8.
7. A. James, *Retrospect of a military life during the most eventful periods of the last war: Journal of Sergeant James Anton 42nd Highlanders* (W. H. Lizars, Edinburgh, 1841), pp.190-5.
8. William Seymour, *et al*, *op. cit.*, pp.200-1.
9. Hamilton-Williams, *op. cit.*, p.216.

'THE GREAT MISTAKE'

When Napoleon inspected the positions of the Anglo-Allied army he declared that he was thoroughly satisfied with the great mistake that Wellington was making by accepting battle in front of the forest of Soignes. So what went wrong?

MAIN PICTURE: A view of the battlefield at Waterloo from Wellington's perspective. He based himself by the crossroads where the Braine l'Alleud–Ohain road crossed the Brussels to Genappe highway, next to an elm tree which can be seen in this painting.

(All Images Courtesy of Anne S.K. Brown Military Collection, Brown University Library unless otherwise stated)

Though Wellington had held the crossroads at Quatre Bras, the Prussians had been beaten at Ligny. The failure of d'Erlon's Corps to intervene at Ligny had prevented Napoleon achieving the crushing blow he hoped for, but, nevertheless, the Prussians had been badly beaten and had been forced to withdraw.

On learning of Blücher's defeat at Ligny, and of his subsequent retreat, Wellington also had to withdraw. By mid-morning on 17 June, the Anglo-Netherland's infantry had started to fall back along the Brussels road, covered by the artillery and cavalry. Napoleon, who had joined Ney at Quatre Bras, ordered an attack upon the crossroads at a little after 13.00 hours. He was too late – only a rear-guard remained.

Any possibility of a vigorous pursuit was ended because of a sudden and dramatic change in the weather. 'A storm, such as I had never seen the like of, suddenly unleashed itself on us and on the whole legion,' recalled Lieutenant Jacques Martin of the French 45th Line Regiment. 'In a few minutes the road and plain were no more than a swamp which became still more impracticable for the storm persisted and lasted the rest of the day and the whole night. Men and horses sank into the mud up to their knees. The growing darkness prevented troops from seeing each other, battalions mingled and each soldier marched as best he could and where he could. We no longer formed an army but a real crowd.'[1]

LEFT: The regiments which formed the Household Cavalry Brigade consisted of the Life Guards, the Royal Horse Guards and the 1st Dragoon Guards. Here can be seen the Royal Horse Guards on the left and the 1st and 2nd Regiments of the Life Guards.

By 18.00 hours on the 17th, Wellington's wet and muddy force had reached the place that Wellington had earmarked earlier – the ridge of Mont St Jean to the south of the village of Waterloo. While the Mont St Jean was not a severe obstacle to the attacking forces, it held distinct advantages to the defenders. The first of these was that Wellington was able to conceal a large part of his army behind the crest of the ridge so that Napoleon could only guess at the Allied dispositions. By the same token, the higher position provided Wellington with a good view of the French, which would give him early warning of any move by them. It also meant that the British and Allied troops could shelter behind the crest of the ridge from the French artillery, which considerably outnumbered that of the Allies. We are led to believe that Wellington had earlier reconnoitred the area and, having seen the Mont St Jean position, he allegedly claimed 'I have kept it in my pocket' just in case Napoleon attempted to seize Brussels from the south-east.

Wellington's Anglo-Netherlands force was stationed to the north of a track running east from Braine l'Alleud towards Ohain along a low ridge close to the village of Mont St Jean. This road was cut along the ridge and was usually described as a 'sunken' road. Troops stationed on the road would be very well protected from enemy fire. The ridge crossed the main Charleroi to Brussels road at right angles. The entire line was less than two miles long, which meant a heavy concentration of force, giving the defenders strength in depth.

The position was also buttressed by three significant strong points. The Château d'Hougoumont was on the front right of the Allied line, with the farmhouse of La Haye Sainte, which stood by the Charleroi-Brussels road, immediately in the Allied front. Lastly, on Wellington's left flank were the farms of Papelotte and La Haye and, beyond these, the château of Frichermont. These stood at the foot of Mont St Jean, acting as redoubts ahead of the Allied position.

The troops had bivouacked overnight close to the positions they were to take up during the battle, though at daybreak there was some re-adjustment as the regiments moved to their assigned places in the line. →

LEFT: An officer of the Royal Engineers. Lieutenant Colonel Carmichael Smyth of the Engineers, acting on Wellington's instructions, had made a survey of the Mont St Jean position in 1814 which helped the Allied force take up its positions when it arrived on the 17th.

ABOVE: A painting of the Battle of Waterloo from a sketch made on the spot by Dennis Deighton.

RIGHT: The 23rd Light Dragoons were with the 3rd British Cavalry Brigade and was stationed in reserve behind Wellington's right centre.

BELOW LEFT: On the evening of 17 June 1815, Napoleon and his staff installed their headquarters in this building, Caillou farmhouse, spending the night there on the eve of the battle. The farmhouse has now been transformed into the Napoleon Museum.

FAR RIGHT: This ossuary, located in the grounds of Caillou farmhouse, was erected in 1912. It contains the remains of soldiers killed at Waterloo in 1815. These bones were found on parts of the battlefield.

The Throw of the Dice

Across the low valley to the south Napoleon's army had also gathered during the night. The Emperor was happy with Wellington's decision to stand and fight. The Duke's multi-national army would be crushed that day and the coalition of nations would collapse. 'France,' declared Napoleon, 'was going to rise, that day, more glorious, more powerful and greater than ever'.[1] Yet Napoleon was beaten at Waterloo. So exactly what happened 200 years ago on 18 June 1815?

Wellington's 67,661-strong army included 23,991 British troops, with the German states of Hanover, Brunswick, Nassau and the King's German Legion contributing 25,886 men. Dutch-Belgian troops made up the balance. Assembling before them was just two-thirds of Napoleon's army, the remainder having been placed under the command of Marshal Grouchy and sent off in pursuit of the Prussians. Nevertheless, the French army is usually considered to have been a far more formidable force. Though numerically only slightly larger at 72,000 men, it was composed of men who had returned to the colours when the Emperor called – all of whom had fought in at least one campaign. Possibly even more significant was that Napoleon commanded 256 guns, many of which were heavy 12-pounders, compared with just 156 under Wellington's command.

Providing Grouchy, who had been sent with the right wing of the army to pursue the retreating Prussians, could keep Blütcher's troops away from Waterloo, Napoleon was convinced that his force would destroy the Anglo-Allied army. He was 'thoroughly satisfied', as he put it, 'with the great mistake which the enemy general was making'.

The mistake, as Napoleon saw it, was that Wellington had decided not to retreat through the forest of Soignes in the hope of joining up with the Prussians in front of Brussels. If Wellington had done exactly that it would have presented Napoleon with a considerable problem. It would have meant the French army defiling through the forest to exit in line of march in the face of the Allied guns. Such a move also allowed more time for Blücher to join Wellington. Finally, by offering battle at Mont St Jean, Wellington had the forest at his back. If the Allied army broke, there would be no easy retreat through the forest.

'The enemy general,' declared the Emperor, 'could do nothing more at variance with the interests of his cause and his country, to the whole spirit of the campaign, and even to the most elementary rules of war, than to remain in the position which he occupied'.[2] It would not be a defeat, it would be a slaughter. Wellington had thrown his dice, the emperor told Ney, 'and our number has turned up'.

However confident Napoleon might be, he knew that time was not on his side. Though he expected Grouchy to make sure that the Prussians were unable to join Wellington, the marshal's comparatively small force could not be expected to hold back the entire Prussian army indefinitely. Napoleon had therefore wanted to open the battle at 09.00 hours as soon as his men were in position, but the heavy rain of the previous day had delayed the troops, some of whom by this time were

LEFT: French artillery on the move. Napoleon began his military career in the Royal French artillery and his use of such weaponry on the battlefield was a feature of his tactics. Rather than placing his artillery in immediate support of the infantry, as was traditional, Napoleon massed his guns in order to blast a hole in the enemy's line. This tactic was repeated at Waterloo with his grouping of 80 guns into a 'Grand Battery'.

only beginning to assemble into their allotted positions. The artillery was experiencing even greater difficulty dragging its guns through the mud. Nevertheless, the day had broken fine and clear, and the ground was drying rapidly. In another couple of hours or so, the gunners declared, the big guns would be ready.

Plan of Attack

After inspecting the Allied position, which in truth he could see little of because so many of Wellington's men were out of sight behind Mont St Jean, Napoleon 'reflected' for a quarter of an hour before giving his orders for the attack. These called for Reille's II Corps, which was drawn up to the west of the Charleroi-Brussels road, to advance upon the Allied right while d'Erlon's I Corps would attack the positions to the east, or the Allied left. The cavalry was formed up on either wing and in immediate support behind each infantry corps, with the Imperial Guard in reserve on both sides of the road ready to intervene when and where required.

Shortly afterwards Napoleon made a slight alteration to these orders. The attack upon the Allied right was merely to be a diversionary move with the attack by I Corps, on the Allied left, being the decisive one, as he described: 'I had preferred to turn the enemy's left, rather than his right, first, in order to cut it off from the Prussians who were at Wavre, and to oppose their joining again, if they had intended doing so, if the attack had been made on the right, the English army, on being repulsed, would have fallen back on the Prussian army; whereas, if made on the left, it would be separated therefrom and thrown back in the direction of the sea; secondly, because the left appeared to be much weaker; thirdly and finally, because I was expecting every moment the arrival of a detachment from Marshal Grouchy on my right, and did not want to run the risks of finding myself separated from it.'[3]

This was an entirely sound plan, based on the information Napoleon had at the time. It was certainly the case that Wellington's force to the east of the Charleroi-Brussels road was the weakest and the left flank was open and exposed. It almost appeared as if he was inviting an attack in that direction. Had Wellington made yet another mistake?

Wellington was aware of the danger which was posed by giving battle in front of the forest. He was also extremely concerned about his right flank. If Napoleon was able to turn that flank he would be able to cut Wellington off from the Charleroi-Brussels road, his only line of retreat. To add to those concerns, a strong force of French cavalry had ridden down the Mons to Brussels road to the west of Waterloo during the night. Though the French cavalry had rejoined the main body, this implied that Napoleon was considering a wide sweep around →

BELOW LEFT: The farm of La Belle Alliance at Waterloo, as seen in the 1920s. This building, which doubled as an inn, became Napoleon's headquarters for the Battle of Waterloo. (Historic Military Press)

BOTTOM LEFT: Farm de Mont St Jean was situated to the rear of the Allied positions and was used as a field hospital during and after the battle. (Historic Military Press)

BOTTOM RIGHT: A view of the courtyard of Farm de Mont St Jean as it appeared in 1909. (Historic Military Press)

ABOVE:
Battle is joined on the Mont St Jean. In the centre can be seen the Prince of Orange mounting his horse and accompanied by his staff.

the Allied positions with the aim of encircling Wellington's force.

This worried Wellington so much that, as we have seen, he concentrated the bulk of his army between the Nivelles-Brussels and the Genappes-Brussels roads. He also posted part of his II Corps at the town of Hal (or Halle) eight miles away to the west on the Mons-Brussels road. This consisted of a Netherlands Division under Prince Frederick of the Netherlands and part of the Anglo-Hanoverian Division of Lieutenant General Colville, and amounted to some 17,000 men and 30 guns. This was a very considerable proportion of his force to subtract when he was facing the bulk of the French Army led in person by one of the greatest military commanders the world had ever known.

Yet Napoleon had no intention of attempting any complex flanking manoeuvres. He believed that he had Wellington exactly where he wanted him.

Opening Shots

It would be Reille's corps that would open the battle. This, Napoleon hoped, would encourage Wellington to send reinforcements to that side and, in doing so, limit the extent to which he could support his left wing when the main French attack was delivered upon that weaker flank.

When the various divisions had formed up ready for the attack Napoleon rode along their ranks. 'It would be difficult to express the enthusiasm which animated all the soldiers,' Napoleon later wrote, 'the infantry raised their shakos on the ends of their bayonets; the cuirassiers, dragoons and light cavalry, their helmets or shakos on the ends of their sabres. Victory seemed certain.'

At sometime between 11.30 and 11.50 hours (opinions vary) one of Reille's batteries opened fire upon the Château d'Hougoumont. As the first attack was being delivered against Hougoumont, the so-called 'Grand Battery' opened fire with all of its 80 guns at midday which would precede the main attack upon Wellington's left. This battery consisted of 42 six-pounders, 18 12-pounders and 20 howitzers. The battery was deployed for about three-fifths of a mile along the ridge south of the Mont St Jean, which made it difficult for the French cannon to hit the British regiments on the reverse slope and impossible for the French gunners to see their targets.[4]

Wellington ordered his men, who were already sheltering behind the crest of the ridge, to lie down to further reduce the effect of the French shot. Even so, as Sergeant Robinson of the

BELOW:
This illustration by Alexander Sauerweid Pinx gives some indication of the confusion and chaos of the fighting.

FAR RIGHT:
An officer of the Netherlands Militia in 1815. Wellington chose to intersperse the Netherlands and Hanoverian brigades with the more experienced British brigades so that no part of his line was weaker than any other.

92nd Regiment, remembered: 'At this time, our men were falling fast from grape shot and shells that the French were pouring in amongst us, while as yet we had not discharged a musket.'[5]

For 90 minutes this cannonade continued: 'A number of staff officers were soon killed & wounded who were at first alone exposed to the cannonade,' wrote Major Stanhope of the 1st Foot Guards. 'General Cooke lost his arm, shells began to fall in our squares & though many men were blown up & horribly mangled I never saw such steadiness. As the poor wounded wretches remained in the square it was a horrid sight in cold blood.'[6]

At 13.30 hours Napoleon considered that the guns had sufficiently softened up the enemy and he ordered Ney to begin the great attack.

Into The Attack

Though the battle was only two hours old, and it was still early afternoon, Napoleon was becoming increasingly worried. This was because he had

received some disturbing news from Colonel Marbot, whose 7th Hussars had been ordered to send patrols as far east as the River Dyle to watch for the possible appearance of either the Prussians or Grouchy. Marbot's men had captured a Prussian courier carrying a letter from Gneisenau to von Müffling and now that messenger was presented to the Emperor. The letter said that the bulk of Bülow's IV Prussian Corps would soon reach Chapelle St-Lambert, only around three miles away!

Napoleon and his staff turned their telescopes to the east. 'The troops you see are the advance guard of General von Bülow,' said the courier. 'Our whole army passed the night at Wavre. We have seen no French, and we suppose they marched on Placenoit.'[7] But there was no sign of Grouchy at Placenoit or anywhere else.

CHIEF OF STAFF

Marshal Soult was Napoleon's chief of staff during the Waterloo campaign and it was his job to interpret Bonaparte's instructions into orders for each subordinate commander to follow. As there was much uncertainty and confusion at times during the campaign it cannot be said that Soult did a particularly good job of what was a new role for him.

What had happened to Grouchy? Why had he not stopped the Prussians from marching on Mont St Jean? Possibly at this stage Napoleon began to doubt his verdict on Wellington's actions. The Emperor had believed that the Duke had committed a grave error in giving battle in front of the Forest of Soignes. Now it seemed that Wellington had not been so unwise after all. But what was it that Wellington knew that Napoleon didn't?

On the afternoon of the 17th Wellington had told Blücher that he intended to make a stand at the Mont St Jean provided he was supported by one Prussian corps. 'But if this support is denied me,' he continued, 'I shall be compelled to sacrifice Brussels and take my position behind the Scheldt'. In other words, if Blücher did not join him at Waterloo, Wellington would retreat to the coast leaving the Prussians to face Napoleon alone.

At 22.00 hours on the evening of 17 June, a Prussian messenger had arrived at Wellington's headquarters with Blücher's reply. 'I shall not come with one corps only, but with my whole army; upon this understanding, however, that, should the French not attack us on the 18th, we shall attack them on the 19th.'

Later, at 02.00 hours on the morning of the 18th, another message was received from Blücher, in which he went even further in his commitment to support Wellington: 'Bülow's Corps [IV Corps] will set off marching at daybreak tomorrow [the 18th] in your direction. It will be followed immediately by the corps of Pirch [II Corps]. The I and III Corps will also hold themselves in readiness to proceed in your direction.'[8]

Wellington now knew that he was going to be joined by the entire Prussian Army which would be on the road at daybreak. It would not be Wellington's army alone that Napoleon would be facing, but the combined might of both Allied armies.

Everything that Napoleon had achieved by separating Wellington and Blücher and defeating the Prussians at Ligny had been thrown away. A great mistake had been made by giving battle at the Mont St Jean, but it was not Wellington who had made it.

ABOVE: An officer of the 42nd Foot, the Black Watch. The 42nd was with Major General Sir Denis Pack's 9th British Brigade.

LEFT: The King of Britain was also Elector of Hanover, and Hanoverian troops formed a considerable part of Wellington's army. This is a trooper of the Bremen and Verden Hussars.

NOTES:

1. J. Martin, *Souveneirs d'un ex-officier* quoted in Andrew Uffindell and Michael Corum, *On the Fields of Glory, The Battlefields of the 1815 Campaign* (Greenhill, London, 1996), p.30.
2. Somerset de Chair, *Napoleon on Napoleon: An Autobiography of the Emperor* (Brockhampton Press, London, 1992), p.256.
3. *Ibid*, p.262.
4. Jeremy Black, *The Battle of Waterloo, A New History* (Icon, London, 2010), pp.100-101.
5. D. Robertson, *Journal of Sergeant D. Robertson Late 92nd Foot comprising the different Campaigns, 1797 and 1818, in Egypt, Denmark, Sweden, Portugal, Spain, France, and Belgium* (J. Dewar, Perth, 1842), p.154.
6. Gareth Glover, (Ed.), *Eyewitness to the Peninsular War and the Battle of Waterloo: The Letters and Journals of Lieutenant Colonel James Stanhope 1803 to 1825 Recording His Services with Sir John Moore, Sir Thomas Graham and the Duke of Wellington* (Pen & Sword, Barnsley, 2010), p.176.
7. David Hamilton-Williams, *Waterloo New Perspectives, The Great Battle Reappraised* (Arms and Armour, London, 1993), p.282
8. Captain W. Siborne, *History of the Waterloo Campaign* (Greenhill Books, London, 1993), p.174.

THE BRAVEST MAN AT WATERLOO

The crucial defence of Hougoumont played a huge part in the outcome of the battle – and led to a unique bequest to one soldier made by a rural Suffolk clergyman.

MAIN PICTURE: Sergeant James Graham, Coldstream Guards, the bravest man at Waterloo, shown carrying his brother to safety. (Anne S.K. Brown Military Collection, Brown University Library)

ABOVE: A view of the South Gate today, site of the first attacks on Hougoumont and where Bauduin was the first of Napoleon's generals to die during the battle. (Courtesy of Paul Hermans)

The large farmhouse known as Château d'Hougoumont was a key component of Wellington's defensive line and had to be held at all costs. The château complex, a working farm, consisted of the main house surrounded by farm buildings joined by a high wall. Beyond this was a garden, orchard and a not inconsiderable wood.

'The farm is well calculated for defence,' wrote Lieutenant Colonel (later Lieutenant General) Alexander Woodford of the Coldstream Guards. 'The dwelling house in the Centre was a strong square building, with small doors and windows. The barns and granaries formed nearly a square, with one door of communication with the small yard to the South [i.e. facing the French] and from that yard was a door into the garden, a double gate into the wood, under or near the small houses, which I conclude you call the Gardener's house; and another door opening into the lane on the West. There was another carriage gate at the North-West angle of the great yard, leading into the barn, which conducted to the road to Braine-le-Leud *[sic]*'.[1] This northern gate was to acquire great significance later.

Such was the importance of Hougoumont, Wellington placed there troops whom he could rely upon – the Guards. Consequently, the light company of the 2nd Battalion Coldstream Guards was stationed in the farm and château, with the light company of the 2nd Battalion, Third Guards, in the garden and grounds, and the two light companies of the 2nd and 3rd Battalions of the First Guards in the orchard. The Guards were supported by the 1st Battalion, 2nd Nassau Regiment, with additional detachments of *jägers* and *landwehr* from von Kielmansegge's 1st (Hanoverian) Brigade.

Command of Hougoumont was entrusted to Lieutenant Colonel James Macdonnell of the Coldstream Guards. The place had been fortified as much as was possible in the few hours before the first shots of the Battle of Waterloo rang out. The walls had been loopholed, platforms had been built and tiles had even been removed from the roof to allow men to fire down upon attackers.

The Assault Begins

It was the artillery of General Reille which fired the first shots on the British positions, marking the start of the assault upon Hougoumont in a contest that would last all day. Reille gave the task of attacking Hougoumont to Prince Jérôme Bonaparte's 6th Division. Napoleon had no interest in taking such a strong position, all he expected of his younger brother was that he would draw into the struggle for the château as many British troops as possible so that when

NEAR RIGHT: General, later Field Marshal, John Byng commanded the 2nd Guard's Brigade.

FAR RIGHT: The interior of Hougoumont during the battle. On the right is the chapel and on the far right is the entrance to the orchard and wood. (Anne S.K. Brown Military Collection, Brown University Library)

the Emperor delivered his main assault upon the centre-left of Anglo-Allied line Wellington would have no reserves to call upon.

The first attack was delivered by General Baron Bauduin's 1st Brigade supported by two batteries of horse artillery. The French *tirailleurs* ran into the woods with bayonets fixed, but were halted by the fire of three companies from the Nassau regiment and the Hanoverian *jägers*, some 600 men in total. Increasing numbers of French were thrown into the wood and the defenders withdrew, disputing every tree and bush.

It took an hour for the French to clear the wood. They had suffered heavy losses, with Bauduin just one of many officers killed or wounded. This was as far as Jérome's men were supposed to go. With the wood in French hands, Reille could bring up the rest of his force hidden by the trees. But the men of the 1st Brigade, seeing themselves only 30 yards from the château and lacking the officers to restrain them, charged across the open ground. They were cut down by heavy fire from the Guards and driven back into the wood.

An Overwhelming Force

Though the attack upon Hougoumont was only intended to be a diversionary move, Jérôme persisted with his attack, hoping, it would seem, to actually seize the château, though this was beyond his orders. Despite the fact that he had already lost around 1,500 men from his 1st Brigade, he then threw his 2nd Brigade at Hougoumont. Almost 8,000 men were now tied down by less than half that number.

Seeing what appeared to be an overwhelming force committed to taking Hougoumont, Wellington responded. With the British artillery was a troop of the Royal Horse Artillery equipped solely with howitzers, and Wellington asked Major Bull if his gunners could lob their shells into the wood without hitting the Guards who were behind the adjacent walled garden. In ten minutes the French were driven from the wood under the accurate fire of Bull's six guns. The defenders then advanced and re-took part of the wood.

As the attack upon Hougoumont had been blunted without Wellington being required to move any of his reserves across to his right, Napoleon ordered Reille to send another division against the château. The 2nd Brigade of General Foy's 9th Division marched round the eastern side of Hougoumont but was unable to swing round the flank of the château complex because it was met by General Byng's 2nd Guards Brigade. The increased pressure on Hougoumont did finally compel Wellington to commit some of his reserves, in the form of a battalion of Hanoverians and three battalions of the Brunswick corps. Now more than 4,000 men held the château and the buildings against one and-a-half French divisions.

With the Allied troops once again in the wood, Bull had to stop his howitzers for fear of hitting men of his own side. This allowed the French to push increasing numbers into the wood, especially against the northern side of the château. There a few men from the Light Companies of the Coldstream and Third Guards were posted outside the walls. They were attacked by Jérôme's light troops, and in the fighting a haystack caught fire behind them. With the French bearing down on them the Guards could see that they were in danger of being cut off and so they

BELOW LEFT: Jérôme Bonaparte commanded the French 6th Division which was given responsibility for attacking Hougoumont and drawing down Wellington's reserves. (Anne S.K. Brown Military Collection, Brown University Library)

BELOW RIGHT: The Lion Mound (in the distance) seen beyond the southern wall of Hougoumont's Formal Garden. It was this wall that stood between the British, German and Dutch defenders against the might of the French 2nd Corps. If this wall had been breached during the fighting at Hougoumont, the outcome of the Battle of Waterloo could have been different. (Courtesy of Paul Hermans)

quickly withdrew through the northern gate back into the courtyard of the château. The gate had been left open to allow troops to pass between the château and its grounds.

Closing The Gate

The guardsmen now tried to close the gates. But a number of men of the French *1er Régiment d'Infanterie Légère*, led by *Sous-Lieutenant* Legros, managed to force their way into the courtyard. Legros was a giant of a man and had been given the nickname *L'Enfonceur.* With, apparently, a heavy axe, he forced back the gates and his men followed.

Lieutenant Colonel Macdonnell, who was also a big man, threw himself at the gates. This was the critical moment of the fight for Hougoumont. If Macdonald could close the gates, the château might yet remain in British hands, but if more French poured into the courtyard, Hougoumont would be lost and with it the whole of Wellington's right flank would be exposed.

Seeing the danger, two burly Guard NCOs, Corporal James Graham of the Coldstream and Sergeant McGregor of the Third Guards, rushed to help Macdonnell. Others ran to assist, including Graham's brother. Gradually they pushed the gates shut and James Graham slammed a heavy cross-bar into position. They then barricaded the gates with ladders, posts, barrows and anything that came to hand.

TAKING THE BRICK

The actions of Graham and Macdonnell at Hougoumont are still commemorated by the Coldstream Guards in a unique ceremony – the Hanging of the Brick. Each year, depending on where the battalion is serving, the ceremony takes place on a date in December before Christmas.

The night before the ceremony, a genuine brick taken from the wall of Hougoumont is secured by a sturdy chain in the Guardroom.

The next day, members of the Sergeant's Mess, in fancy dress, with the Corps of Drummers at their head march to the Guardroom to collect the brick.

Tradition then states that the brick is paraded around the battalion by the Sergeants' Mess (and Corps of Drums) arriving at the Officers' Mess where the commanding officer and all officers are invited to attend the traditional activities in the Sergeants' Mess.

On the way round though, guardsmen and lance corporals are invited to try and 'take' the brick. If they do so, then they can 'hold it ransom' to the Sergeants' Mess who must pay for beer and drinks all day in the Junior Ranks Bar to release it. Needless to say, every effort is made by the junior ranks to capture the brick.

The French continued to hammer away at the gates but could not break through, and the 20 or so of Legros' party inside the courtyard were killed with the exception of one drummer boy. Legros died still clutching his axe.

Though Hougoumont itself had been secured, the French light infantry held the grounds. They were driven back from the garden wall by a bayonet charge of four companies of the Coldstream Guards under Lieutenant Colonel Woodford that had been sent by General John Byng (who commanded the 2nd Guards Brigade) when he saw how desperate the situation was becoming at Hougoumont.

Woodford then entered the courtyard by the small gate on its west side, his men then adding to the strength of the garrison.

Foy responded by sending in his last brigade. This was spotted by either General von Alten or by Wellington and more troops were sent to help the now surrounded defenders of Hougoumont. The French were forced out of the garden, leaving them in possession only of the orchard.

ABOVE LEFT: Nassau infantry charging the French. The Duchy of Nassau was an independent state in what are now the German states of Rhineland-Palatinate and Hesse. (Anne S.K. Brown Military Collection, Brown University Library)

LEFT: Hougoumont's North Gate, which, attacked by the French 1st Légère, was defended by British Guards. (Courtesy of Paul Hermans)

FAR RIGHT: **An NCO and Grenadier of the Coldstream Guards in 1815.** (Anne S.K. Brown Military Collection, Brown University Library)

BELOW RIGHT: **The memorial to the men of the Coldstream Guards at Hougoumont.** (Courtesy of Paul Hermans)

BELOW RIGHT: **One of the last remaining trees of the original wood at Hougoumont – stripped of its bark and riddled with holes by musket shot – by Hougoumont's South Gate.** (© 2007–8 Frank Toogood)

BELOW: **Another painting of Hougoumont after the battle.** (Anne S.K. Brown Military Collection, Brown University Library)

Hougoumont On Fire

Later in the day, a shell landed in the large barn, 'and the smoke and flames burst out in a most terrible manner', Woodford later wrote, 'and communicated with rapidity and fury to the other buildings. Some officers attempting to penetrate the stables to rescue some wounded men, were obliged to desist, from the suffocation of the smoke, and several men perished.'

It was at this time that James Graham asked his colonel for permission to fall out. Sergeant Graham's Company was holding the garden wall that had been taken by Colonel Woodford. Knowing Graham's courage, Macdonnell was surprised by such a request and asked why. Graham explained that his brother, Joseph, had been wounded and was lying in one of the buildings that was on fire. He wanted to leave the ranks so that he could rescue him. Graham promised that he would return to his Company as soon as he had removed his brother to a place of safety.

Macdonnell agreed. Graham dashed into the blazing building and dragged his brother from the fire. He laid him down in a ditch at the rear of the château enclosure and, true to his word, returned to his position on the wall. It is also said that at one point in the battle Graham also saved the life of Captain Wyndham – one of those who had helped shut the gate – by shooting a French soldier whose musket was trained on the officer.

Hougoumont remained in Allied hands all day, its defenders inflicting thousands of casualties upon the enemy and tying down such a large proportion of Reille's divisions as to effectively prevent II Corps from fully contributing to the battle. Wellington was well aware of this and after the battle he declared that 'the success of the battle turned upon closing the gates at Hougoumont'. In the defence of Hougoumont the Coldstream Guards lost more than 300 officers and men. James Graham was promoted to the rank of sergeant for his bravery. He also received a special medal from his regiment and an annuity.

The Bravest Man

In August, while the Anglo-Allied army was still in occupation of Paris, the Duke of Wellington received an extraordinary letter from the Reverend Mr Norcross, rector of Framlingham, Suffolk. Rev. Norcross declared his intention of rewarding the most deserving soldier at the battle by passing on the income from a freehold farm. This amounted to £10 per annum. The grant was for life. The clergyman asked if Wellington would make the choice on his behalf.[2]

The Duke asked Sir John Byng to choose someone who had distinguished himself in the defence of Hougoumont. Byng chose Sergeant Graham. This was announced in brigade orders of 9 August 1815. Graham thus became, officially, the bravest man at Waterloo.

Unfortunately for James Graham, the rector got into financial difficulties and the annuity only lasted for two years.

Although the rector died in 1837 it was reported in a number of books and newspapers that he had recovered his fortunes enough to leave £500 in his will to 'the bravest man in England'. Wellington was, once more, the man who would make the nomination. Again Wellington turned to Hougoumont, this time selecting Colonel Macdonnell. It was said that Macdonnell split the bequest with Graham, since they had shut the gate together. This story of a second bequest, though, remains unsubstantiated.

NOTES:

1. H. T. Siborne, *Waterloo Letters* (Greenhill Books, London, 1993), pp.263-4.
2. Captain W. Siborne, *History of the Waterloo Campaign* (Greenhill Books, London, 1995), pp.238-9.

'THIS DISASTROUS RESOLVE'

As the battle unfolded, both Napoleon and Wellington knew that the Prussians held the key to victory. With the exact messages now available for examination, the most challenging question of the Waterloo campaign can be answered – was it Marshal Grouchy or Napoleon himself who failed to keep the Allied armies separated?

Napoleon was confident that he could win the battle on the Mont St Jean. All he needed to do was make certain that the Prussians did not join forces with the British. To make sure that this happened he had divided his army, sending approximately a third of his force to pursue Blücher and keep him heading away from Wellington.

The task of pursuing the Prussians was entrusted to Marshal Emmanuel de Grouchy. Unlike almost all of Napoleon's generals, Grouchy was the son of an aristocrat but he had fought almost continuously with the French Army since 1779 and distinguished himself in battle after battle. It is usually said that the task now given to him was beyond his capabilities as, until then, he had never commanded anything larger than a cavalry corps.

Yet all that was expected of him was to keep the Prussians from joining the British. With a lifetime of warfare behind him, most of it in fairly senior positions, such a job should have been well within his grasp.

Nevertheless, this was his first quasi-independent command and, as the French historian Houssaye observed, Grouchy was not comfortable with such responsibility: 'From the first instant Grouchy felt the burden, rather than the honour, of this mission.' Almost every historian has criticised Grouchy's conduct.

Grouchy could be relied upon to follow Napoleon's instructions quite closely, especially as this was his first large multi-arm independent command. Everything then depended on the instructions given to him by the Emperor – the most critical orders of the entire campaign.

Pursue The Enemy

Napoleon did actually discuss his instructions with Grouchy and in his memoirs he stated that 'he had a definite order to remain throughout between the road from Charleroi to Brussels and Blücher, so as to keep continuously in touch with, and be in a position to join up with, the army'.

This would seem to be clear and precise. However, Napoleon's orders have been preserved and we know exactly what was transmitted to Grouchy. The first of these orders was given to Grouchy at Ligny, timed at 11.00 hours on the 17th:

'Proceed to Gembloux with the cavalry corps of Generals Pajol and Exelmans, the light cavalry of IV Corps (Gérard), the Teste infantry division and the III (Vandamme) and IV Infantry Corps. You will reconnoitre in the direction of

MAIN PICTURE: As Grouchy ponderously follows the Prussians, battle is joined on the Mont St Jean. (Anne S.K. Brown Military Collection, Brown University Library)

ABOVE: Étienne Maurice Gérard commanded the IV Corps and was the man who famously insisted that Grouchy should march to the sound of the guns over at Waterloo. He later became French Prime Minister. (Anne S.K. Brown Military Collection, Brown University Library)

Namur and Maastricht and you will pursue the enemy. Scout out his march and inform me of his movements to enable me to penetrate his intentions. I am transferring my headquarters at Quatre-Bras, where the English still were this morning. Our communications will therefore be by the paved road of Namur. If the enemy had evacuated Namur, write to the General commanding the 2nd Military Division at Charlemont in order to have this town occupied by a few battalions of the National Guard. It is important to penetrate Blücher's and Wellington's intentions and to know whether they propose to re-unite their armies to cover Brussels and Liége by tempting fate in a battle. In any case, keep your two infantry corps constantly together in two and a half miles of ground with several retreat exits; post intermediary cavalry detachments to communicate with General Headquarters.'

Though fairly detailed, nothing in these instructions actually stated that Grouchy must make sure the Prussians should be prevented from joining Wellington. Furthermore, quite how Grouchy was expected to penetrate Blücher's and Wellington's intentions is a mystery. Nevertheless, Grouchy set off in pursuit of Blücher with around 30,000 men, Napoleon having reduced his force by subtracting a division of infantry and one of cavalry.

At 22.00 hours on the 17th, Grouchy sent his first report from Gembloux, though it was not received at Napoleon's headquarters until 04.00 hours on the 18th: 'Sire, the enemy, 30,000 strong, continue to retreat. It seems from all reports that, from Sauvenières, the Prussians have divided into two columns. One must have taken the road to Wavre through Sart-a-Walhain, the other seems to have taken the direction of Perwès [Liége]. A third one, with artillery, is retreating on Namur. One can infer that a portion is going to join Wellington and that the centre, which is Blücher's army, retreats on Liège. If the Prussians' mass retires on Wavre, I shall follow it in this direction to prevent it from reaching Brussels and to separate it from Wellington. If on the contrary, their principal forces have marched on Perwès I shall follow them in pursuit through this town.'

This despatch clearly shows that Grouchy fully understood his instructions and he declared that he would follow the Prussian column to 'separate it from Wellington'. The despatch indicated that part of the Prussian force was attempting to meet up with Wellington and that another column was heading away along the Prussians' natural line of retreat. This meant that only a proportion of Blücher's force was heading to Wavre and on to Waterloo. This was very good news. All Napoleon had to do was to say to Grouchy that if the main Prussian force was marching on Liége he should let them go. As Napoleon himself once famously said, never interrupt your enemy when he is making a mistake.

GROUCHY

Following the events at Waterloo, Marshal Emmanuel de Grouchy spent the rest of his life defending himself and his actions. There was even an attempt to have him condemned to death through a court-martial, though this failed. Exiled, he lived in America until 1821, when he returned to France.

RIGHT: French troops, including infantry and artillery, assemble. (Anne S.K. Brown Military Collection, Brown University Library)

Grouchy had appeared to have done very well. He had, seemingly, divined Blücher's intentions which indicated that he was moving with at least part of his force to join Wellington. There was no longer any point in Grouchy following Blücher. All Grouchy's force would be needed at Waterloo.

Establishing Contact

This is Napoleon's reply to Grouchy from his post at Caillou, which, written by Soult, was timed at 10.00 hours: 'You talk to His Majesty of two Prussian columns which have passed at Sauvenières and Sart-a-Walhain. However, some reports say a third column, quite a strong one, passed through Géry and Gentinnes marching towards Wavre. The Emperor enjoins me to warn you that at this moment he is about to have the English army attacked at Waterloo near the Forest of Soignes where it has taken up position. His Majesty therefore desires that you should direct your movements on Wavre so as to come nearer to us, to establish operational and liaison contact with us, pushing in front of you the Prussian army corps who have taken this direction and who might have stopped at Wavre, where you must arrive as soon as possible. You will have the Prussian army corps who have taken to your right followed by some light corps so as to observe their movements and to gather their stragglers. Instruct me immediately of your dispositions and of your march as well as of the information you possess on the enemy, and do not neglect to bind your communications with us. The Emperor desires to have news of you very often.'

The seeds of failure have been sown here by Napoleon. He last learnt that Grouchy was at Gembloux. He instructs Grouchy to march on Wavre. A simple look at the map shows that if Grouchy followed Napoleon's instructions he could not possibly prevent the Prussians from joining the Anglo-Allied army at Waterloo. Napoleon was going to be severely outnumbered. This message was, according to Dr David Chandler, neither a clear order of recall, nor a definite order to continue independent action.[1]

The only possible chance of saving the situation was if Grouchy could move so rapidly that he would overtake the Prussians. Merely pushing the Prussians in front, by its very definition, would mean that the Prussians would reach Waterloo before Grouchy.

Speed was therefore of the essence, but Napoleon waited six hours before sending the despatch to Grouchy. This delay has been attributed by many historians to Napoleon's health. →

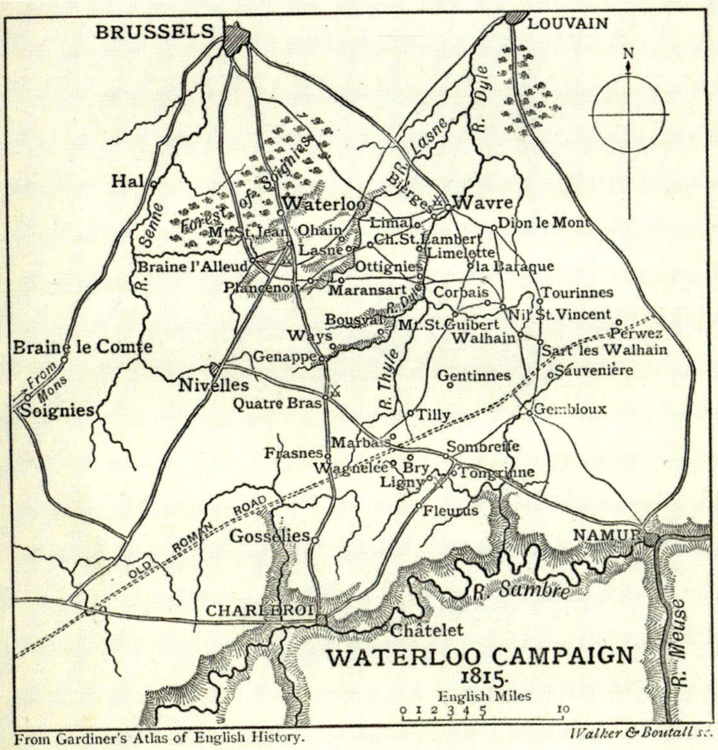

LEFT: A map of the campaign area, showing some of the key locations relating to 16, 17 and 18 June 1815.

MIDDLE LEFT: *Général de division* Rémi Joseph Isidore Exelmans commanded the French II Cavalry Corps.

BELOW: The guns of Napoleon's Grand Battery open fire on the Anglo-Allied line. This battery was among the first to open on Wellington's forces, and therefore among those that Marshal Emmanuel de Grouchy and General Gérard heard. (Anne S.K. Brown Military Collection, Brown University Library)

TOP LEFT: **Prussian cavalry study a map while on the march – it was men such as these whom Grouchy was pursuing.** (Anne S.K. Brown Military Collection, Brown University Library)

TOP RIGHT: ***Général de division* Rémi Joseph Isidore Exelmans commanded the French II Cavalry Corps.**

He appears to have suffered bouts of lethargy and utter exhaustion during the course of the campaign due to an illness called Acromegaly.[2]

There was no such excuse for Grouchy who had allowed the Prussians to escape in the night, as his despatch of 06.00 hours reveals. 'Sire, all my reports and information confirm that the enemy is retiring on Brussels to concentrate there or to give battle after joining Wellington. I and II Corps of Blücher's army seem to be marching, the first on Corbais, the second on Chaumont. They must have started yesterday evening (17 June) at 8pm from Tourinnes and marched all night; fortunately the weather was so bad that they cannot have gone very far. I am leaving this instant for Sart-a-Walhain and from there to Corbais and Wavre.'

Bad weather or not, the Prussians had many hours start on Grouchy. There was no way he could now overtake the Prussians in time. This message was received at Rossomme at 11.00 hours, just as the Battle of Waterloo was about to begin.

Intercepted Order

It was still possible for Napoleon to save the day. It was taking about four hours for a message to reach its destination, though Grouchy was now moving closer. An immediate instruction could be sent to Grouchy telling him to march directly upon Waterloo which would be received at, or quite possibly before, 15.00 hours. Though finding suitable roads would be difficult, Grouchy might yet be able to influence the outcome of the battle, with sunset not being until around 21.00 hours. But Napoleon did not reply immediately. His next instruction to Grouchy was not until 13.15 hours. Two-and-a-quarter hours had been lost.

That despatch, again written by Soult, includes the following: 'The Emperor orders me to tell you that you must always manoeuvre in our direction and seek to come closer to us in order to join us before any corps can come between us.' At last, the correct instructions had been sent, but it was far too late.

In his memoirs Napoleon paints a somewhat different picture. 'At ten o'clock in the evening [of the 17th], I sent an officer to Marshal Grouchy whom I supposed to be at Wavre, in order to let him know that there would be a big battle next day … I ordered him to detach from his camp at Wavre a division of 7,000 men of all arms and 16 guns, before daylight, to go to Saint-Lambert to join the right of the Grand Army and co-operate with it.'

There is no record of such a despatch in Soult's register, though it is possible that not every instruction was recorded. There is anecdotal evidence, from Blücher's son, that a French staff officer was captured (or had deserted) and taken to his father's headquarters. He claimed that 'he was carrying an order written in pencil addressed to Marshal de Grouchy saying that the latter must march on the point where the Emperor was and leave 6,000 men in front of the Prussian Army so as to mask his movements and to keep the enemy in check whilst making his move'. With that information in his hands, Blücher made exactly the move that Grouchy was instructed to make and ordered his army to march upon the French right flank at Waterloo.

Disastrous Resolve

This may or may not be true, but Napoleon could have expected to have received confirmation of this from Grouchy in the morning of the 18th. However, the early morning message from Grouchy makes no mention of detaching any troops to join Napoleon.

This should have sent alarm bells ringing in Napoleon's head and he should have responded immediately by sending an urgent message to Grouchy to join him at Waterloo at all costs. As we know, he didn't. He excuses himself by stating that he believed Grouchy's claim that the hours lost during the night would be made up in the morning and that by 'starting at daylight, in order to arrive early in front of Wavre, which would come to the same thing [as marching through the night], and that the men would be well rested and full of dash'.

At that time Napoleon did not question Grouchy's reasoning, nor, as we have seen, did he urge him to march directly upon Waterloo. Nevertheless, in his memoirs Napoleon places all the blame on Marshal de Grouchy, who, the emperor wrote, 'sent out reconnaissance parties in the two directions of Wavre and Liège on the tail of the two enemy rear-guards, which had retired that way. This done, Grouchy made his troops take up their position.

'He had, however, only covered two leagues. Towards evening he received definite information to the effect that the principal units of the army were making for Wavre, but it was after six o'clock, and the men were just making their soup. He thought he would be in time next day to follow the enemy, who were thus found to have gained three hours on him. This disastrous resolve is the principal cause of the loss of the Battle of Waterloo.'[3]

It is true that Grouchy did not strain every muscle to keep his sword in Blücher's back, though he still seems to have believed that his forces could block the Prussians attempting to move beyond Wavre. After riding up to III Corps to check on its progress, he sat down to a late breakfast, a little after 11.00 hours, after writing the following despatch: 'The I, II, and III Prussian Corps, under Blücher, are marching towards Brussels. Two of these corps marched through Sart-à-Walhain, or passed just to the right of the place; they marched in three columns roughly keeping abreast of each other … One Corps coming from Liège [Bülow's IV], effected its concentration with those that had fought at Fleurus … It would seem as though they intend to give battle to their pursuers [Grouchy's force], or finally to join hands with Wellington; such was the reports spread by their officers, who, in their usual boasting spirit, pretend that they only left the field of battle on June 16 [Battle of Ligny] in order to ensure their junction with the English army at Brussels. This evening I shall have massed my troops at Wavre and thus shall find myself between the Prussian Army and Wellington, who, I presume, is retreating before Your Majesty.'[4]

Following Orders

Everything seemed to indicate therefore that the British and Prussians were going to fall back upon Brussels. Grouchy had no reason to believe that Wellington would be making a stand at Waterloo until it was too late. Although he had not been vigorous in his pursuit, as long as he put himself between Wellington and Blücher he would have carried out the task allotted to him. Because Napoleon had waited six hours before replying to Grouchy's earlier despatch, the latter did not know that a great battle was about to begin just a few miles away.

Hardly had Grouchy finished this despatch and sat down to breakfast when the sound of cannon fire was heard to the west. General Gérard immediately urged the Marshal to cancel his current arrangements and march without delay to the sound of the guns. 'Marshal, it is your duty to march to the cannon,' Gérard insisted. Grouchy was not impressed at being told by a subordinate what his duty was. 'My duty,' he replied, 'is to execute the Emperor's orders, which direct me to follow the Prussian. It would be infringing his commands to pursue the course of action which you recommend.'[5]

Grouchy has been almost universally condemned for this. It is a military axiom that no general can do wrong if he marches to the sound of the guns. But for all that Grouchy knew, what could be heard might be a rearguard action by the Anglo-Allies as they fell back upon Brussels. If Grouchy abandoned his pursuit of the Prussians to join Napoleon he might, in that case, permit Wellington and Blücher to join hands in front of the Belgian capital.

What, though, was most probably foremost in Grouchy's mind was the criticism that Napoleon had levelled against Ney when he had deviated from his orders on the 15th. Ney had sent his infantry off towards the sound of the guns instead of pressing on towards Quatre-Bras. The Emperor had made himself clear that night over supper. Grouchy was not going to fall into that trap. He had his instructions and he was going to stick to them.

The result was that the Prussians stayed ahead of him and were already bearing down on Waterloo. Grouchy said that his duty was to follow Napoleon's instructions, but those instructions, as we have seen, were garbled and confusing. It was not Grouchy who failed his master, it was the Emperor himself who let victory slip away from him.

ABOVE: Prussian cavalrymen, more specifically Hussars, prepare to advance. (Anne S.K. Brown Military Collection, Brown University Library)

LEFT: *Général de division* Pierre Claude Pajol commanded the French I Cavalry Corps under Grouchy. (Anne S.K. Brown Military Collection, Brown University Library)

BOTTOM LEFT (FACING PAGE): A Prussian officer of Dragoons. (Anne S.K. Brown Military Collection, Brown University Library)

NOTES:

1. David Chandler, *The Campaigns of Napoleon*, *op. cit.*, p.1067.
2. A.F. Becke, *Napoleon and Waterloo* (Greenhill, London, 1995), pp.276-80.
3. Napoleon, *op. cit.*, p.99.
4. Grouchy to Napoleon, Sart-les-Walhain, 11 a.m., 18 June 1815, quoted in Hamilton-Williams, *op.cit*, pp.313-4.
5. Becke, *op. cit.*, p.250.

LAST STAND AT LA HAYE SAINTE

History tells of many famous valiant defences against overwhelming odds: Thermopylae, The Alamo, Rorke's Drift. The defence of a small farm complex by a few hundred men at Waterloo can be ranked in a similar category.

MAIN PICTURE: Massed columns of French infantry attack Mont St Jean. (Anne S.K. Brown Military Collection, Brown University Library)

Grouchy's failure to impede the march of the Prussians meant that by early afternoon Blücher's force was bearing down on Napoleon's right flank in front of Mont St Jean. Yet there was time enough for Napoleon to beat the British. The leading Prussian Corps (Bülow's IV Corps) was still an hour's march away and it would take even longer for his force to deploy fully. His advance could be further delayed by transferring some of the French reserves. Though even Napoleon had admitted that the odds against him had lengthened, all

was not yet lost. Reille was ordered to increase pressure upon Wellington's right around Hougoumont as the great attack by I Corps was delivered.

At 13.30 hours Ney was given the word, and with the beating of the *pas de charge* from hundreds of drums and the excited calls of '*Vive l'Empereur!*', the great French mass moved forward. They advanced in an unusual formation, with the 1st Division on a two company frontage behind which were the 2nd, 3rd and 4th Divisions in battalion columns, which meant a battalion in line followed by each battalion in the division close behind (just three paces) also in line. As each division consisted of 12 battalions these battalion columns would have been about 200 yards wide by 40 yards deep. Ahead of d'Erlon's entire corps was a swarm of skirmishers consisting of the light companies from each division.

Directly in the path of these massive formations, almost 20,000 men in total, was the farmhouse of La Haye Sainte. The dwelling-house of the farm, the barn, and stables were surrounded by a rectangular wall beyond which to the south, i.e. towards the direction of the advancing French columns, was an orchard encompassed by a hedge. To the north was a kitchen-garden which was defined by a wall on the road side and a hedge on the other three sides. There were two doors and three large gates in the courtyard wall, though one of these had been broken down and used as firewood by the troops. →

LEFT: A rifleman of the 2nd Light Battalion, King's German Legion, which was posted in La Haye Sainte from the outset of the battle. (Anne S.K. Brown Military Collection, Brown University Library)

ABOVE: As the fighting raged in and around La Haye Sainte, the Prince of Orange, with Belgian troops, attacked the French positions to the right of the farm. (Anne S.K. Brown Military Collection)

RIGHT: Lieutenant Colonel Konrad Ludwig Georg Baring was in command of the defence of La Haye Sainte. The King's German Legion was dissolved after Waterloo and Baring joined the newly formed army of the Kingdom of Hanover.

TOP RIGHT: A non-commissioned officer of the French cuirassiers, which played an important part in the fighting at La Haye Sainte. (Anne S.K. Brown Military Collection, Brown University Library)

The King's German Legion

Major Baring, with between 380-400 men of the 2nd Light Battalion King's German Legion, had been given just a few hours to try and put La Haye Sainte into a defensible state before the battle began. His pioneers, though, had no equipment, the mule that carried the entrenching tools having been lost in the confusion of the retreat from Quatre-Bras. The pioneers had to go over to Hougoumont to get hold of the implements they needed.

'We had no loopholes excepting three great apertures, which we made with difficulty when we were told in the morning that we were to defend the farm,' explained Lieutenant G.D. Graeme. 'We had no scaffolding, nor means of making any, having burnt the carts, etc. [for firewood]. Our loopholes, if they may be thus termed, were on a level with the road on the outside.'[1] An abatis was also placed across the road a little in the front of the farm's main gate, behind which the defenders could stand and which would further hinder the French advance.

The men were still working on the farmhouse's defences when the first French attack began, and the door on the western side of the farm, the one which had been used as firewood, had not been properly barricaded. Baring placed two of his six companies in the building block, another in the garden at the rear, or northern side of the farm, with the remaining three companies in the orchard. In fairly close support were three companies of the 1st Battalion, 95th Rifles in a sand-pit to the north of the farm enclosure. The farm lay in a hollow, so to be able to observe the movements of the enemy Baring placed himself in the orchard. 'Shortly after noon, some skirmishers commenced the attack,' he later recalled. 'I made the men lie down and forbade all firing until the enemy were quite near.'[2]

'En Avant!'

Amongst those men of the King's German Legion (KGL) was Rifleman Friedrich Lindau. 'First, about midday, the thunder of the French cannon rolled towards us,' he later recalled. 'We stood ready to fire behind the hedge and waited for the enemy. It was not long before a swarm of enemy skirmishers came, a thousand rifles [*sic*] exploded and a jubilant cry '*en avant!* resounded; behind them were two columns of enemy troops of the line who marched forwards so quickly that we said to one another: "The French are in such a hurry, it's as if they wanted to eat in Brussels today."'

The La Haye Sainte farm complex, in the centre front of the Allied position, disrupted the advance of I Corps, and

95TH RIFLES

An officer of the 95th Rifles. Three companies of the regiment's 1st Battalion occupied a sandpit to the north of the farm enclosure during the battle for La Haye Sainte. As the King's German Legion was part of the British Army, its uniforms were almost identical to those worn by British soldiers of the same respective branch of the service. The riflemen of the 1st and 2nd Light Battalions of the KGL were therefore dressed in the same 'rifle' green as the 95th. The dark green colour and black accoutrements worn by riflemen represented an early attempt at camouflaged clothing. (Anne S.K. Brown Military Collection, Brown University Library)

it was soon all but surrounded by the 2,000 men of the 1st Brigade of d'Erlon's 1st Division.

'Now the enemy stood at the entrance to the barn,' continued Lindau, 'we drove them back and went inside, admittedly with many casualties. Then we gave such unbroken fire in the barn behind – towards the open entrance – in front of which the French were thickly massed, that they did not attempt to enter.'

Lindau held his ground here for around 30 minutes before the French, through sheer weight of numbers, drove him back. He then moved to one of the loopholes near the farm's main gateway where he claimed that the French were so closely packed together that on more than one occasion he saw three or four of them shot through by one bullet.

It seemed that at any minute the little garrison of the farm would be overcome. Seeing Baring's predicament, Count Kielmansegge, in command of the 1st Hanoverian Brigade, sent the Light Battalion Lüneburg down to help. The Lüneburgers moved down to La Haye Sainte in line. Now reinforced, Baring tried to recover the orchard, and the Germans charged the French at bayonet point (more accurately at sword point as the Baker rifles with which they were armed carried short swords, or hangars, in place of bayonets).

'They did not hold their position as we pressed forward with overpowering boldness,' Lindau later wrote. 'I stabbed and cut blindly into the crowd.'

The Cuirassiers Charge

At this juncture Dubois' Cuirassier Brigade of the IV Cavalry Corps rode up in support of d'Erlon's infantry. The Lüneburgers were taken by surprise by the sudden appearance of the cavalry and instead of forming square they ran back up the ridge from where they had come, taking with them some of the KGL, including Baring himself. The three companies of the 95th, now completely isolated, and seeing the Germans running back to the main Allied position also abandoned the sandpit and rushed up the ridge.

ABOVE: The 1st King's Dragoon Guards formed part of the British heavy cavalry that charged into d'Erlon's Corps. (Anne S.K. Brown Military Collection, Brown University Library)

LEFT: An officer (with sword) and rifleman of the 2nd Light Battalion King's German Legion. (Anne S.K. Brown Military Collection, Brown University Library)

The Germans were cut to pieces by the heavy French cavalry as they tried to escape, leaving just a few men of the KGL, under the command of Lieutenants Marenholtz, Voigt and Westernhagen, in La Haye Sainte. Though completely outnumbered and surrounded, the light infantry held on to the farmyard and buildings.

While La Haye Sainte had disrupted d'Erlon's attacking columns it could not stop them and the French infantry pushed on up the slope of Mont St Jean. They were pounded by the Allied artillery which had been placed on the crest of the ridge, but as they closed upon the Allied line Bylandt's Belgian brigade came under accurate and heavy fire from the leading French ranks and fell back. This left a gap in the Allied front line which was quickly plugged by two brigades of Picton's 5th Division.

More French battalions reached the ridge, the Allied gunners abandoning their guns. The British infantry, 3,000-strong, unleashed a stunning volley, but still the French came on. Nothing, it seemed, could stop the massed blue columns and as they mounted the top of the hill they shouted 'Victory'.

At that moment, the Earl of Uxbridge launched his heavy cavalry. The squadrons of the Household Brigade and the Union Brigade, more than 2,000 sabres, crashed first into the French cuirassiers and then into the packed ranks of the French infantry.

I Corps was driven back all along the line which allowed Baring to re-occupy La Haye Sainte. Baring asked for some support and two companies of the 1st →

LEFT: A drawing of La Haye Sainte as viewed from the Allied positions. (Courtesy of Extraordinary Editions)

ABOVE LEFT: A depiction of the storming of La Haye Sainte, in a painting by Richard Knötel.

TOP RIGHT: The plaque on the outer wall at La Haye Sainte which commemorates the endeavours of Major Baring and the men of the King's German Legion.

ABOVE RIGHT: Another of the memorials on the outer wall at La Haye Sainte. This one remembers the French infantry and engineers who assaulted the valiantly-held farm on Ney's orders.

Light Battalion KGL were sent to help him. These he deployed in the garden, leaving the farm building in the hands of the three tough lieutenants who had defied the French for so long.

A Desperate Battle

The charge of the British cavalry gave Baring about 30 minutes respite, during which time d'Erlon's men regrouped and recovered. At around 15.30 hours, the French Grand Battery began another bombardment. It was the prelude to another attack, and this time the objective was to clear the Allies out of La Haye Sainte, which was severely obstructing the attack upon the main Allied line.

Once again the French moved in columns towards the farm. They advanced, Baring later wrote, 'with the greatest rapidity, nearly surrounded us, and despising danger, fought with a degree of courage which I had never before witnessed in Frenchmen. Favoured by their advancing in masses, every bullet of ours hit, and seldom were the efforts limited to one assailant.'

The accurate fire of the rifle-armed light battalions did not stop the French throwing themselves against the walls of the farm; some of them even grabbed hold of the rifles through the loopholes the Germans had made in the walls of the buildings. The French also pushed their muskets through the loopholes and fired inside. A desperate battle was fought around the main gate which the French saw as a weak point. Baring claims that he counted 17 dead Frenchmen piled up on that very spot.

It was now mid-afternoon and still La Haye Sainte defied the enemy. Worst still from Napoleon's perspective was that the Allied positions on the ridge of Mont St Jean remained intact. The minutes were slipping by; Napoleon had to do something to break the Allied line and secure victory.

He had the Imperial Guard in reserve but he wanted to hold them back for the decisive moment when the Allies began to waver. His infantry had so far achieved little, but the cuirassiers had proven to be highly effective, as had the British cavalry. So the cavalry it had to be. There was no point in piecemeal attacks, it would have to be every available horseman.

The Emperor handed Ney the honour of winning the battle. 'It could not be entrusted to a braver man, nor to one more accustomed to this kind of thing,' declared Napoleon. 'I sent orders to Marshal Ney to open fire with his batteries, to get hold of the farm of la Haie-Sainte [*sic*] and to put an infantry division in there … Eighty pieces of artillery belched forth death upon the whole of the English line.' As the bombardment subsided, 5,054 cavalry charged towards La Haye Sainte.

'As they marched upon the position of the farm,' recorded Baring, 'I brought all the fire possible to bear upon them; many men and horses were overthrown, but they were not discouraged. Without in the least troubling themselves about our fire, they advanced with the greatest intrepidity … The contest in the farm continued with undiminished violence, but nothing could shake the courage of our men, who, following the example of their officers, laughing, defied danger.'

The Squares Stand Firm

I Corps had also been ordered to take La Haye Sainte and they were determined to seize the farm. 'New regiments were continually brought up but regularly beaten back,' Rifleman Lindau boasted. 'An enemy officer fell to me nearby; he had been constantly riding round the battlefield in front of us and showing

RIGHT: The farm of La Haye Sainte, from the south-east corner, as it appeared in the 1920s. (Historic Military Press)

LEFT: La Haye Sainte today. Note the various memorials and plaques on the walls. Today, it is privately owned as a family home. To the left of the image is the the main gate of La Haye Sainte where Frederick Lindau and his comrades battled to keep the French at bay. It was finally smashed down as the defenders ran out of ammunition.

BOTTOM RIGHT: The end wall of the farmhouse on the Charleroi-Brussels road. The building has not changed to any great extent since it played a very important part in the fighting on 18 June 1815. The road leads from La Belle Alliance, where Napoleon located his headquarters on the morning of the battle, through where the centre of the French front line was located, to a crossroads on the ridge and then on to Brussels.

BOTTOM LEFT: A drawing originally published in 1817, depicting La Haye Sainte after the battle. (John Grehan)

the way to the advancing columns. For some time I had him in my sights – at last, just as he was leading up new troops, he came into my fire. His horse made a bound, reared up and fell with the rider beneath it.'

Ney launched his cavalry at the Allied line, but the British, Dutch, Belgium and German infantry were prepared and quickly fell into battalion squares, an almost impenetrable formation. Wave after wave of cuirassiers, lancers and chasseurs swarmed round the squares but were unable to break them. The British light cavalry counter-attacked and the French squadrons were driven back. The Allied gunners, who had run into the nearest squares when the French horsemen had rushed up the ridge, returned to their guns and poured canister into the retreating cavalry.

Witnessing the failure of the cavalry, the infantry of I Corps also withdrew. The defenders of La Haye Sainte had, once again, defied the odds.

Baring had his horse shot from under him during this latest attack – for the second time – but his battalion had suffered fewer casualties than in the first attack. That was not the case with the attackers, and Lindau recalled seeing heaps of dead French soldiers lying on and near the road by the abatis.

The men of the light battalions of the King's German Legion now experienced a period of respite. During that time Baring sent an officer to request more ammunition as his men, armed with rifles not muskets, were down to about half the cartridges they had started the battle with.

For about an hour the men were able to rest, but then La Haye Sainte was attacked with even greater ferocity than before. No ammunition had been received and when he saw the French approaching Baring sent another officer with an urgent appeal. Though no ammunition was forthcoming, Baring at least received reinforcements in the form of the Light Company of the 5th Line Battalion KGL. Baring yet again sent a message back for more rifle cartridges and once more received no ammunition, only further reinforcements, on this occasion some 200 men from the two flank companies of the 1st Nassau Regiment.

Fire!

This time the French concentrated their efforts at the entrance to the barn, but still the Germans stood firm. The shortage of ammunition, however, was becoming a real problem and as soon as a man went down, the others rummaged through his pockets searching for cartridges.

Despite all their efforts, the French could still not break into the farm by force, so they tried another method – setting fire to the barn. It seemed that the Germans were going to be driven from the barn but luckily the Nassau troops had brought their camp kettles →

RIGHT: The farmhouse where the men of the King's German Legion made their heroic stand, as seen from inside the main wall.

BELOW RIGHT: This diamond-shaped commemorative plaque can be found on the end wall of the farmhouse at La Haye Sainte. It was presented by the officers of the 2nd Light Battalion King's German Legion in honour of their 'comrades-in-arms who fell in the defence of this farmhouse on the 18 June 1815'.

BOTTOM LEFT: Pictured in the 1920s, these monuments are located next to La Haye Sainte. On the left is the Hanoverian (King's German Legion) Memorial. (Historic Military Press)

BOTTOM RIGHT: Unveiled in 1965, this memorial commemorates those French personnel who gave their lives in the fighting on this part of the Waterloo battlefield.

with them and these were used to bring water from the farm pond. Yet, by leaving their posts to fight the fire, the men had left loopholes unoccupied.

The French began to fire through the loopholes, so Lindau, by this time having been wounded twice in the head, and a few others, ran back to their positions. 'Then just as I had fired,' recounted Lindau, 'a Frenchman seized my rifle to snatch it away. I said to my neighbour, "Look, the dog has seized my rifle."'

'"Wait," he said, "I have a bullet," and at once the Frenchman fell. At the same moment another seized my rifle, but my next man on the right stabbed him in the face. I needed to draw my rifle back to load it, but a mass of bullets flew by me, rattling on the stone of the wall. One took the worsted tuft from my shoulder. Another shattered the cock on my rifle.' Lindau ran back to where one of his comrades was dying and took the man's rifle.

Baring's men defied the French for a further one-and-a-half hours, but after the enemy had withdrawn, a count of the ammunition available revealed that there were only three or four rounds per man left. He knew that the next attack would be the last one.

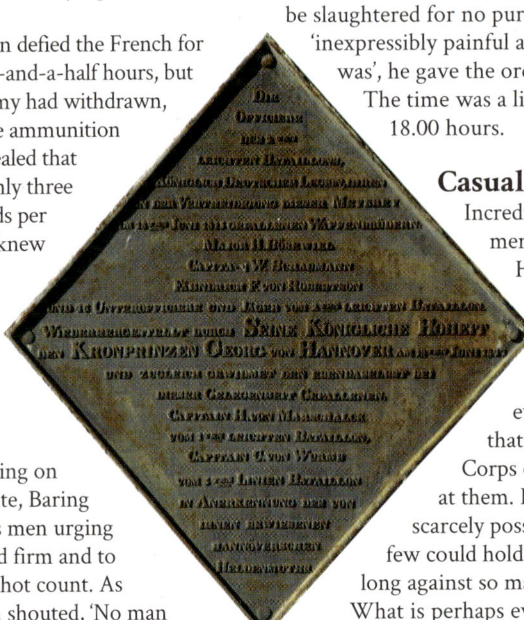

When he saw the French once more advancing on La Haye Sainte, Baring addressed his men urging them to stand firm and to make every shot count. As one, the men shouted, 'No man will desert you, we will fight and die with you.'

The determination of the Germans counted for little when their ammunition finally ran out. As the fire from the farm diminished, the French broke into the farmyard, while others climbed onto the roofs and walls of the buildings. Eventually, Baring had to accept that by remaining in the farm with no ammunition his men would be slaughtered for no purpose and 'inexpressibly painful as the decision was', he gave the order to retreat. The time was a little after 18.00 hours.

Casualties

Incredibly, Baring's men had held La Haye Sainte for four-and-a-half hours against everything that the French I Corps could throw at them. It seems scarcely possible that so few could hold out for so long against so many.

What is perhaps even more remarkable is that the KGL only gave up their defence of the farm after they had run out of ammunition. Their courage, though, came at a price – the 2nd Battalion of the King's German Legion suffered almost 90% casualties.

At the end of the fighting, the exhausted troops slept on the battlefield. Baring recounted his feelings that night: 'Of the 400 men with which I had entered the battle I now had no more than 42. According to who I could ask, the answers came: dead! – wounded! – I freely admit that I instinctively wept tears at this news and also at so great a bitterness I felt helplessly take possession of me. I was roused from these sad thoughts by the general-quartermaster of our division, Major Shaw, who was my trusted friend. I felt exhausted in the highest degree and my leg was very painful; with my friend I lay down in some straw, which the men had gathered for us to sleep on. On waking, we found ourselves between a dead man and a dead horse.'

NOTES:

1. Major G.D. Graeme's letter, in H.T. Siborne, *Waterloo Letters* (Greenhill Books, London, 1993), pp.406-9.
2. North Ludlow Beamish, *History of the King's German Legion*, Vol.II, (Buckland and Brown, London, 1993), pp.453-62.
3. The Lindau quotes are taken from *A Waterloo Hero, The Reminiscences of Friedrich Lindau*, which is edited and presented by James Bogle and Andrew Uffindell and was published by Frontline Books in 2009.

SNARING THE EAGLES

During the charge of the Union Brigade at Waterloo two Imperial Eagles were captured, to be later laid at the feet of the Prince Regent. But who captured these great symbols? We investigate a 200-year-old mystery.

D'Erlon's Corps, almost 16,000 strong, in vast, dense columns, was marching directly at the thin Anglo-Dutch line. Though their order and impetus was broken by the farm of La Haye Sainte and its stubborn defenders, nothing, it seemed could stop the massed French infantry.

The 1st/95th, in the sandpit in front of La Haye Sainte, fell back to the main Allied position, leaving Bylandt's 1st Netherland's Brigade to confront the advancing enemy. Battered by the French skirmishers – the *chasseurs* and *voltigeurs* – and then blasted by a powerful volley from the head of one of the columns, the Dutch troops also fell back upon the second line. A dangerous gap had opened up in the centre of the Allied positions.

Appreciating the danger, Lieutenant General Sir Thomas Picton, in command of the British 5th Division in the second line, ordered two of his brigades forward. His 8th Brigade met one of the French columns and halted it with its controlled fire. The 9th Brigade, under Major General Pack, also moved forward but unexpectedly found itself facing *Général de Division* Marcognet's entire 3rd Division. Pack's men had moved up in column and, taken by surprise, were unable to deploy into line before the French opened fire. The enemy then followed up with the bayonet.

'We drove them back at the point of the bayonet,' wrote Captain Duthilt of the French 45th Line Infantry Regiment, 'and climbed higher up the slope and over stretches of quick hedge which protected their guns. Then we reached the plateau and gave a shout of 'Victory'.'[1]

It certainly seemed at this point that the French infantry was on the point of breaking through the Anglo-Netherlands line and, with their cavalry waiting to exploit such a breakthrough, the battle looked to be reaching its climax.

At this point, Lieutenant General Henry Paget, the Earl of Uxbridge, in charge of the Anglo-Dutch Cavalry Corps, made possibly the most important decision of his military career. Included in his command were two brigades of heavy cavalry. One was the Household Brigade, which included the Life Guards, the Horse Guards and the 1st Dragoon Guards, and the other was called the Union Brigade as it included regiments from England, Ireland and Scotland. Paget ordered the whole of his heavy cavalry to charge.

Charge of the Heavies

The Household Brigade led the way, smashing into the French cavalry on the infantry's flank. The Union Brigade then struck d'Erlon's great columns of infantry. Caught before they could form square, the French were slaughtered. →

MAIN PICTURE: The taking of the Eagle of the French 45th Line. Throughout the entire Waterloo campaign, only two French Eagles were captured during battle, both by the Union Brigade in this particular action. (Anne S.K. Brown Military Collection, Brown University Library)

ABOVE: The 2nd (Royal North British) Dragoons were all mounted on white horses and therefore came to be called the Scots Greys. It was usual, where circumstances permitted, for regiments to be mounted on horses of the same colour. (Anne S.K. Brown Military Collection, Brown University Library)

'In vain our poor fellows stood up and stretched out their arms; they could not reach far enough to bayonet these cavalrymen mounted on powerful horses,' continued Captain Duthilt, 'and the few shots fired in chaotic mêlée were just as fatal to our own men as to the English [*sic*]. And so we found ourselves defenceless against a relentless enemy who, intoxicated of battle, sabred even our drummers and fifers without mercy.'

The British cavalry penetrated so far into the ranks of the French battalions that Sergeant Charles Ewart of the Scots Greys, part of the Union Brigade, managed to seize one of the prized Imperial Eagles. As he cut his way through the blue-coated infantry he found himself just a short distance from the Eagle of the 45e *Régiment de Ligne*. He made for the Eagle but three men threw themselves in his way.

'One made a thrust at my groin,' Ewart recalled. 'I parried him off and cut him down through the head. A lancer came at me – I threw the lance off by my right side and cut him through the chin and upwards through the teeth. Next, a foot soldier fired at me and then charged me with his bayonet, which I also had the good luck to parry, and then I cut him down through the head.'

As Ewart rode away with the Eagle he had another narrow escape, for a wounded Frenchman, who he had taken for dead, raised himself up on one elbow and fired at him as he passed. The ball fortunately missed him and he was able to take his prize, proudly, to the rear.

Attack The Colour

The 1st (Royal) Dragoons experienced similar success. They struck the head of *Général de Brigade* Baron Charles-Francois Bourgeois' 2nd Brigade. The column, at the head of which was the 105e *Régiment de Ligne*, was driven back some 200 yards by the Dragoons.

Leading one squadron of the Royals was Captain Alexander Kennedy Clark Kennedy (at the time of the battle known as Kennedy Clark): 'I gave the order to my Squadron, "Right shoulders forward, attack the Colour," leading direct on the point myself. On reaching it, I ran my sword into the Officer's right side a little above the hip joint. He was a little to my left side, and he fell to that side with my left hand, but could only touch the fringe of the flag, and it is probable it would have fallen to the ground, had it not been prevented by the neck of Corporal Styles' horse, who came up close on my *left* at the instant, and against which it fell. Corporal Styles was Standard Coverer; his post was immediately behind me, and his duty to follow wherever I led.

'When I first saw the Eagle I gave the order, "Right shoulders forward, attack the Colour", and on running the Officer through the body I called out twice together, "Secure the Colour, secure the Colour, it belongs to me". This order was addressed to some men close to me, of whom Corporal Styles was one. On taking up the Eagle, I endeavoured to break the Eagle from the pole with the intention of putting it into the breast of my coat; but could not break it. Corporal Styles said, "Pray, sir, do not break it," on which I replied, "Very well, carry it to the rear as fast as you can, it belongs to me."'[2]

This all seems quite clear, or was Kennedy Clark protesting just a little too much, and what prompted him to write repeatedly that the Eagle was his? Well this note, actually a letter, was written in 1839 – almost two-and-a-half decades after the battle. Immediately after Waterloo, Corporal Francis Styles, like Sergeant Ewart, was promoted from the ranks to become an ensign. But there was no immediate promotion for Captain Kennedy Clark, despite appealing to the army establishment no less than ten times!

Kennedy Clark's repeated statements that he was the one who captured the Eagle of the 45th have led to almost every one of the thousands of books written about the battle supporting his version of events. Yet, at the time, it was Styles who received the credit. Kennedy Clark believed that it was because he was wounded twice after the taking of the Eagle, causing him to be moved to Brussels where he spent two months recovering – he was therefore not able to give his account of the taking of the Eagle until it had already

RIGHT: The 6th (Inniskilling) Dragoons charging. (Anne S.K. Brown Military Collection, Brown University Library)

FAR RIGHT: The Earl of Uxbridge. He was struck by a cannonball during the battle while close to the Duke of Wellington: 'By God, sir, I've lost my leg!' Uxbridge exclaimed. 'By God, sir, so you have!' replied Wellington. (Anne S.K. Brown Military Collection, Brown University Library)

been believed that it was Styles who had earned that honour.

Colonel Clifton (who was in charge of the Royals at the start of the battle and who was subsequently acting brigade commander) wrote to his immediate boss, Colonel Felton Hervey, soon after the battle. He was not prepared to accept that Kennedy Clark was solely responsible for seizing the Eagle, stating no more than 'the latter's conduct contributing to a great degree to the capture of the Eagle'.

Styles' Claim

Looking for someone to support his claim, Kennedy Clark wrote to the man who had taken over the 1st Dragoons from Clifton, Colonel Dorville. Dorville was another man from the regiment who had received an immediate promotion after the battle. As a result of Clark's persistence, Dorville asked Brigade Major Lieutenant-Colonel Charles Radclyffe to investigate.

Radclyffe asked Styles to provide some evidence to support his claim. As a result Styles wrote to his former troop leader at Waterloo, Lieutenant George Canning, as he claimed that it was Canning who had ordered him to attack the Eagle, not Clark. This is what he wrote to Canning, though Canning's reply no longer exists. Sergeant Styles' letter is dated 31 July 1816 at Ipswich Barracks. It includes the following:

'This day Colonel Clifton did send for me about the taking of the Eagle and the Colour. He asked me if I had any person who saw me take the Eagle. I told him you see me. I believe as the officer of the French was making away with it. I belonged to your troop, at the time and you gave me orders to charge him, which I did and took it from him. When I stated it to him this day, he wants to know the particulars about it and me to write to you for you to state to him how it was. I would thank you to write to the Colonel, as you were the nearest officer to me that day. Sir, by doing so you would much oblige.'[3]

Radclyffe also asked for statements from Privates Anderson and Wilson who had been closely involved in the struggle for the Eagle. Wilson apparently stated that he was to the left of Captain Clark when he thrust his sword into the French officer carrying the Eagle. When it dropped from that officer's grasp, the standard fell across the heads of Anderson's and Clark's horses and against that of Styles. Styles seized it and carried the Eagle off to the rear, accompanied some of the way by Anderson who had been wounded. →

ABOVE: Lady Butler's painting depicting the famous charge by the Scots Greys at Waterloo, 18 June 1815.

LEFT: A British dragoon in 1815. (Anne S.K. Brown Military Collection, Brown University Library)

BELOW: This sketch depicts the moment when the Earl of Uxbridge rode up to his heavy cavalry and ordered them to charge.

ABOVE: **Major General Sir William Ponsonby's brigade charging d'Erlon's infantry.** (Courtesy of Extraordinary Editions)

BELOW LEFT: **The actions of Ensign Ewart at Waterloo were recognised when this public house, a short distance from Edinburgh Castle, was renamed in his honour.** (Courtesy of Kim Traynor)

BELOW RIGHT: **The Eagle captured by Sergeant Ewart is on display in the Royal Scots Dragoon Guards museum.**

Anderson's statement would seem to validate Clark's claim. Wilson, likewise, stated that he heard Captain Clark call out to secure the Colour and he joined Clark in seizing the Eagle. Anderson said that he was only a horses' length to the right of Clark when the latter stabbed the French officer: 'The Colour and Eagle fell against the neck of Corporal Styles' horse who snatched it up and galloped off to the rear.'

Wrong Regiment

Clark's position seemed to be vindicated, or were Anderson and Wilson embittered at the honours bestowed upon Styles, a fellow ranker? Did they feel that Styles had received undue attention when he had played no greater part in the action than themselves?

There is also a strange letter which Clark sent to his sister just a week after the battle while he was still recovering in Brussels. In this he wrote: 'I had the honour to stab the standard bearer of the 45th Battalion of Infantry and take the Eagle which is now in London. It is a very handsome blue flag with a large gilt Eagle on top of the pole with its wings spread.'

What is odd about this letter is firstly that it was the 105th Regiment's Colour that had been taken by the Royals, not the 45th's, and, secondly, his description of the Colour which he calls a blue flag, when, as is well known, the staff of the Eagle carried a Tricolour. It certainly calls into doubt whether he ever actually saw the prize he claimed, let alone captured it.

This is further compounded by a remarkable letter from Lieutenant Colonel F.S. Miller of the other regiment of the Union Brigade, the 6th (Inniskilling) Dragoons, who was a major at the time of the battle. No doubt unaware of the controversy brewing in the 1st Royals, he wrote to Lieutenant General Sir Joseph Straton CB KCH who led the Inniskillings at Waterloo: 'As I perceive the Royals and Greys have an Eagle on their Standards, etc., I think application should be made for the Inniskillings to be granted the same distinction, as I have always considered them as much entitled to it as either the other Regiments.'

Straton replied that: 'My Squadron certainly completely broke one Column, and I always understood, took a number of prisoners, and the Eagle which afterwards got into the possession of one of the other Regiments.'

CORPORAL SHAW

The well-built Corporal Shaw died of his wounds after the battle and so was unable to stake any claim he may have had for capturing an Eagle, though he certainly has his supporters. The National Army Museum's website states that, 'Shaw's training with the regiment and in the ring meant that he excelled at this form of conflict ... However, Shaw's size made him an obvious target. Although surrounded by as many as nine cuirassiers, he fought valiantly many of his opponents before his sword snapped. In desperation he used his helmet to defend himself, but in vain. He was unhorsed and left, terribly mauled, to bleed to death on the battlefield.' His body was recovered after the battle and buried near La Haye Sainte. A few years later Sir Walter Scott arranged for the exhumation and return of the remains to Britain. Scott's fascination with the great man inspired him to retain Shaw's skull in his library at Abbotsford, where it has remained to this day as a rather macabre memento of a legend among men. (Anne S.K. Brown Military Collection, Brown University Library)

Private Penfold

If indeed this is true – and this statement, it will be observed, was not for any personal gain on either officer's part, merely for recognition of the regiment's actions at Waterloo – then the whole question of who captured the Eagle of the 45th is thrown into confusion. If it was the Inniskillings who really captured the Eagle of the 105th, someone surely must know who

LEFT: The Life Guards crashing into the French I Corps. (Anne S.K. Brown Military Collection, Brown University Library)

it was that could claim that honour. Amazingly we know who that person was – Private William Penfold.

'As to Penfold taking an Eagle,' recalled one officer, 'I only know what I *heard* at the time, that he took an Eagle which was by some means dropped or lost, and brought off by a man of the Greys or Royals. But Penn [a Private or NCO of the Royals] says that Penfold *told* him that after we charged he saw an Eagle, which he rode up and seized hold of; that the person that held it would not give it up, and that he dragged him by it for a considerable distance; that the pole broke about the middle and Penfold carried it off; that immediately afterwards he saw Private Hassard engaged by himself, and went to his assistance, giving the Eagle to a young soldier of the Inniskillings, whose name Penn now forgets; and that a corporal of the Royals persuaded that young soldier to let him have it, and he carried it off, and Penn says he *saw* an Eagle broken as described going to Brussels with the prisoners.'[4] Was this Corporal of the Royals none other than Corporal Styles?

All we know of William Penfold is that after being discharged from the army he took over a public house in Brighton which he renamed *The Inniskilling Dragoons*.

This intriguing controversy continues to rage, but after the passage of so many years it is unlikely that we will ever really know who captured the Eagle of 105e *Régiment de Ligne*.

Regardless of these claims and counter-claims, what is certain is that the Union Brigade, little more than 1,100 men strong at the start of the three-day campaign, wrecked d'Erlon's Corps, taking some 2,000 French soldiers captive, with many others killed. The charge, though, cost them dearly, as they lost more than half their number – 616 killed, wounded or missing – mainly because they failed to rally after demolishing the French infantry and in their vulnerable and disorganised state were attacked by a cuirassier brigade and two regiments of lancers.

As for Kennedy Clark, many years later he received his much sought after

BELOW LEFT: By the artist Richard Ansdell, *The Fight for the Standard* dramatically depicts Ewart's capture of the French Eagle of the 45e *Régiment de Ligne*. (Courtesy of Eric Gaba, Wikimedia Commons user 'Sting')

BELOW LEFT: The monument which marks Ensign Ewart's last resting place which can be seen on the Esplanade of Edinburgh Castle. (Courtesy of Jonathan Oldenbuck)

promotion. In 1831 he applied for the Order of the Bath basing his claim on the fact that he captured the Eagle of the 105th. His request was denied. Nevertheless, he continued to work his way through the officer ranks until he was finally made a lieutenant general in 1860. He died four years later.

BOTTOM: Corporal John Shaw of the 2nd Lifeguards in action. Shaw was a well-known and popular pugilist and reputedly killed many Frenchmen during the battle. Tantalisingly, his entry in the *Dictionary of National Biography* states that, 'Shaw then rode at an eagle-bearer, killed him, and seized the eagle. He relinquished it, however, while cutting his way through the foes who immediately surrounded him.' (Anne S.K. Brown Military Collection, Brown University Library)

NOTES:

1. Hamilton-Williams, *op. cit.*, p.297-300.
2. Siborne, *Waterloo Letters*, *op. cit.*, pp.75-6.
3. Mark Adkin, *op. cit.*, pp.416-8, provides a careful and thorough analysis of this controversy, though he does not discuss the claim made by the Inniskilling Dragoons.
4. All of these letters from the Inniskilling Dragoons, are to be found in Siborne, *Waterloo Letters*, *op. cit.*, pp.83-8.

A LOAD OF BALLISTICS

Wellington had little time for the new-fangled military rockets and only allowed a small number to be used at Waterloo. Yet there is some evidence that these few had a considerable influence upon the course of the battle.

The Royal Artillery's Rocket Troop was formed on 1 January 1814. Light and highly mobile, the Rocket Troop was dressed and equipped like the Royal Horse Artillery except that it possessed ammunition, horses and rocket cars instead of guns and limbers. The rocket cars were carriages suitably fitted out to take rockets.

Every gunner carried two holsters, each of which held a 12-pounder rocket. The sticks for the rockets, which were seven feet long, were carried in a bundle on the off-side of the horse. The gunner also carried a small spear-head by which he could transform one of the rocket sticks into a lance.[1]

The man responsible for introducing rockets into military service in Britain was Colonel Sir William Congreve who persuaded the Government to allow him to try them out in action. They were used in boats in the 1805 attack upon Boulogne, a deployment which met with limited success. Two years later, rockets, the largest of which were 42-pounders, had been used to great effect in the Battle of Copenhagen where 40,000 had been fired and caused widespread damage across the city.

Compared with conventional artillery, rockets were highly inaccurate. Against large fortifications and harbours packed with boats the rockets were very useful, but it was an entirely different story when used against formations of troops.

Rockets were used twice in the Peninsular War with little success. They were used against Santarem in 1811, after which Wellington wrote, 'I assure you that I am not a partisan of Congreve's rockets, of which I entertain but a bad opinion.' The rockets were withdrawn but Wellington was offered a rocket troop in September 1813 which he accepted, though he had an ulterior motive for doing so. 'The only reason why I wished to have it,' he explained in a letter to the Earl of Bathurst, 'was to get the horses; but as we are to have them at all events, I am perfectly satisfied. I do not want to set fire to any town, and I do not know any other use of the rockets.'[2] →

MAIN PICTURE: A painting of an exercise conducted with rockets a short time after the defeat of Napoleon. Though the uniforms have changed, the rockets are still the same as those fired at Waterloo.
(All courtesy of Anne S.K. Brown Military Collection, Brown University Library unless otherwise stated)

LEFT: A member of the Rocket Troop with a bundle of rocket sticks.

Sweden's Congratulations

After Napoleon's retreat from Russia in 1813, he was confronted by a powerful multi-national force in October 1813 at Leipzig. The Allied force was mainly composed of troops from Prussia, Russia, Austria and Sweden. Included with the Swedish forces was the Royal Horse Artillery's 2nd Rocket Troop, which was attached to Crown Prince Bernadotte's bodyguard.

A 19th century newspaper article provides an account of the action involving the Rocket Troop: 'The rockets and guns of this battery or troop discharged as a volley some twenty shells and case shot, a mass of fire productive … of the greatest physical and moral effect, partly owing to the novelty of the weapon, partly owing to the appalling noise accompanying the flight of these murderous missiles from the first moment of ignition to that of the explosion of the projectile in the midst of the foe, but most of all from its invisibility during the whole of its flight. Such was the effect of these formidable rockets that a whole brigade became paralysed and surrendered after enduring their fire for only a few minutes. At a very critical point in the Leipzig battle the Crown Prince of Sweden rode up to the commandant and implored him to advance his battery and save the day, as nothing else could; and he did.

'Whereupon, the commandant [Captain Bogue] and his troop advanced rapidly to the village of Paunsdorff, which was held by no less than five battalions, upon whom in advance of the whole army, he opened a most destructive fire. This was at once returned, and a hot combat followed. The French battalions, being unable to withstand the fire, fell into confusion and began to retreat. Captain Bogue charged, the enemy turned, raised their caps, gave three huzzas, and surrendered, some three thousand to the two hundred of the Rocket Troop.'

Every year on the anniversary of the battle the reigning monarch of Sweden still sends greetings to the battery, which is now 'O' Headquarters Battery (The Rocket Troop), Royal Horse Artillery.

ABOVE RIGHT: A member of the Royal Horse Artillery, of which the Rocket Troop was a part.

RIGHT: The Royal Artillery was composed of foot and horse artillery, the latter being expected to function alongside the cavalry. This is a member of the foot artillery, his uniform being styled along the same lines as the infantry, with which the foot artillery normally operated.

Nevertheless, the Rocket Troop was officially brought into existence at the beginning of 1814. After a trial of the weapons, watched by Wellington, an observer wrote in his diary: 'The ground rockets, intended against cavalry, did not seem to answer well. They certainly made a tremendous noise: no cavalry could stand near them if they came near, but in that seemed the difficulty, for none of them went within half a mile of the intended object, and the direction seemed extremely uncertain. I think they would have hit Bayonne, for instance, somewhere or other, and no doubt set fire to the town; but the part of the town you could not very well choose.'

All this convinced Wellington that there was little place for them on the battlefield. 'The effectiveness of the rocket,' he declared, 'is limited to employment against uncivilised natives and Americans'.

Rockets At Waterloo

Among the six Royal Horse Artillery troops provided for the Waterloo Campaign, and attached to the cavalry corps, was the 2nd Rocket Troop commanded by Captain Edward Charles Whinyates. When Wellington learned of its inclusion, he ordered the troop to leave its rockets in storage and to re-equip entirely with 6-pounder field guns. Colonel Sir George Wood, the man in charge of the artillery under Wellington, asked the Duke to reconsider saying, 'It will break poor Whinyates' heart to lose his rockets'. 'Damn his heart, sir!' responded Wellington. 'Let my orders be obeyed.' It would seem, however, that Wellington relented and Whinyates was allowed to take some rockets along with five guns.

That decision paid off on 17 June 1815, during the retreat from Quatre Bras. Uxbridge's cavalry formed the Anglo-Netherlands rearguard along with three horse artillery troops. When eventually pressed by the French, the rearguard withdrew to Genappes. A number of 12-pounder rockets were fired from a 'Bombarding frame', a triangle 'cocked up in the air at an angle of 45°'. The first shot made a tremendous impact by hitting a French gun and scattering some of the accompanying cavalry. This was recalled by H. Mussenden Leathes: 'Success attended the flight of the fiery dart, and a considerable *trouée* [gap] was perceivable in the condensed mass, probably from the novelty of such a pyrotechnique salute'.[3]

The French were evidently astonished with these frightening new weapons, but what happened next was described by Captain Mercer, whose troop was also in the rearguard: 'The order to fire [rockets] was given – port/fire applied – the fidgety missile begins to sputter out sparks and wiggle its tail for a second and then darts forth straight up the road. A gun stands right in its way, between the wheels of which the shell in the head of the rocket bursts, the gunners fall right and left, and, those of the other guns taking to their heels, the battery is deserted in an instant … I saw the guns standing mute and unmanned, while our rocketeers kept shooting off rockets, none of which ever followed the course of the first: most of them, on arriving about the middle of the ascent, took a vertical direction, whilst some actually turned back upon ourselves – and one of these, following me like a squib until its shells exploded, putting me in more danger than all the fire of the enemy.' The rockets clearly terrified Whinyates' gunners and had a similar effect upon the French.

The next day, at Waterloo, the Rocket Troop was positioned on the low ground on the left of the Charleroi-Brussels road. In Whinyates' own account, he states that when the cavalry was moved forwards over the sunken road, Colonel Macdonald in charge of the Horse Artillery ordered Whinyates to move forward. At this point, the sunken road was an obstacle to heavy guns, and so Whinyates was told to leave his guns behind and advance only with his rockets. The troop was told off into 13 Sections, with each Section carrying eight rockets.

At this point precise details are lost, but we do have the accounts of two of Royal Artillery officers. One of these was written by Lieutenant F. Warde who was with Ross's troop of Horse Artillery. The scene he describes is after the British heavy cavalry brigades have smashed into d'Erlon's infantry and the supporting cavalry. The Union Brigade and the Household Cavalry, carried

by the impetus of their charge, over-reached themselves and were quickly surrounded by French cavalry.

The heavies, having suffered severe losses, cut their way through the French ranks and headed back to the safety of their own lines, pursued by the French horsemen. It is at this point that Warde takes up his story:

'Major Whinyates moved at a trot within a range of three hundred yards, and fired volleys of rockets, and in ten minutes the French brigade was in total disorder and dispersed, when a Brigade of French Horse Artillery, consisting of eight pieces of eight-pounders, galloped into action from the rear of the broken Brigade of Cavalry. Major Whinyates then retied upon his guns in the original position ... There were about two hundred and fifty or three hundred rockets used during the commencement of the action.'[4]

It seems highly unlikely that a few rockets could have had such an effect on the enemy as to cause an entire brigade to withdraw. Whinyates himself was more circumspect in his assessment of the situation, declaring only that 'it seems probable that the checking of the Brigade of Enemy's Cavalry must have been about the period the rockets were discharged, but I will not assume nor presume that it was checked by rockets'.

When writing the first major history of the battle, Captain William Siborne wrote graphically of this moment in the action: 'The arena in your front is speedily cleared of both friends and foes – the discharge of rockets, which now attracts your attention appears like a display of fire-works in celebration of the glorious triumph – the affair has terminated.'

We know from the well-documented action at the Battle of Leipzig (see side panel) that infantry was unable to stand when bombarded by these rockets, and from the incident during the retreat from Quatre Bras that these rockets frightened cavalry. Even horses trained to endure musket and cannon fire would be disconcerted with something new and all animals are frightened by fire and flames.

Could it be that the retreating British cavalry was saved from annihilation by Whinyates' rockets, and that because of Wellington's oft-quoted distain for these weapons the incident has been dismissed by historians for the last 200 years?

Perhaps the last word should be given by the unassuming Whinyates himself. These remarks were written in March 1841: 'About five or six years ago I was told that a major of English Dragoons was left wounded near the French line, and that he had said he heard the rockets passing and the French swearing (in their way) at them, and the English for wishing to burn them alive, and that they did not like them at all.'[5]

NOTES:

1. Robert Wilkinson-Latham, *British Artillery on Land and Sea 1790-1820* (David & Charles, Newton Abbot, 1973), p.14.
2. Michael Glover, *Wellington as Military Commander* (Sphere Books, London, 1973), p.224-5.
3. Gareth Glover, *The Waterloo Archive, Volume I: British Sources* (Frontline, Barnsley, 2010), p.110.
4. H.T. Siborne, *Waterloo Letters*, pp.209-10.
5. *Ibid*, pp. 205-6.

ABOVE: Sir William Congreve, the man who introduced rockets into the British Army.

TOP LEFT: The tip of an early Congreve rocket of the Napoleonic Wars which is on display at the Paris Naval Museum.

BELOW: Another painting showing a rocket being fired during a training exercise.

'HARD POUNDING'

It was mid-afternoon and despite repeated French efforts, Wellington's army still stood firm on Mont St Jean. Time was slipping away and Napoleon needed a quick victory. So he turned to his cavalry.

MAIN PICTURE: British infantry in square being attacked by cuirassiers and lancers. (Anne S.K. Brown Military Collection, Brown University Library)

The French cavalry was the most effective, and the most feared, in Europe. Used in mass, it was capable of changing the course of any battle, and had done so many times in the past. Now might be the moment to throw the cavalry at the Anglo-Allied line. Wellington's men had suffered repeated bombardment and had been weakened by the assault of d'Erlon's I Corps. Surely they could not hold out much longer under such pressure?

Napoleon ordered Ney to lead the attack. At his disposal were Milhaud's cuirassier corps and the Light Cavalry Division of the Imperial Guard led by Lèfevre-Desnouettes. In total Ney had a little over 5,000 men. Formidable though this force was, as it moved off with the heavy cavalry in front, waiting on Mont St Jean were 18,000 infantry and 56 guns.

Napoleon ordered his Grand Battery to re-double its efforts in advance of the cavalry attack. 'Never had the most veteran soldiers heard such a cannonade,' observed General Count von Alten in command of the 3rd Division.

The French guns subsided as the massed French cavalry moved off. Captain Mercer of the Royal Horse Artillery was stationed to the rear when the attacks began. 'Suddenly a dark mass of cavalry appeared for an instant on the main ridge, then came sweeping down the slope in swarms, reminding me of an enormous surf bursting over the prostrate hull of a stranded vessel, and then running, hissing and foaming up the beach. The hollow space became in a twinkling covered with horsemen, crossing, turning, and riding about in all directions.'[1]

ABOVE: **The Allied artillery was posted on the forward slope of Mont St Jean. The gunners were ordered to fire at the approaching French cavalry until the very last moment and then run into the nearest infantry square. When the cavalry withdrew, the gunners then ran out of the squares to fire upon the retreating enemy horsemen.** (Courtesy of Extraordinary Editions)

'Vive L'Empereur!'

Watching the French cavalry approach was Ensign Gronow of the 1st Guards: 'Not a man present who survived could have forgotten in after life the awful grandeur of that charge. You perceived at a distance what appeared to be an overwhelming, long moving line, which, ever advancing, glittered like a stormy wave of the sea when it catches the sunlight. On came the mounted host until they got near enough, whilst the very earth seemed to vibrate beneath their thundering tramp. One might suppose that nothing could have resisted the shock of this terrible moving mass. They were the famous cuirassiers, almost all old soldiers, who had distinguished themselves on most of the battlefields of Europe. In an almost incredibly short period they were within twenty yards of us, shouting '*Vive l'Empereur*!'[2]

Such an attack by the French cavalry had been expected and prepared for and the order was given for the infantry to form battalion squares, set out in chessboard fashion to be mutually supporting. The artillery had been placed in front of the infantry on the forward slope of the rise so that that they had a clear field of fire. The gunners had been told to keep firing up to the last possible moment and then rush for safety into the nearest square. In this fashion the infantry waited for the storm to break upon them.

'The formation and advance of that magnificent and highly disciplined cavalry had, as a spectacle, a very grand effect,' wrote James Shaw Kennedy. 'These splendid horsemen were enthusiastic in the cause of Napoleon – full of confidence in him and themselves – thirsting to revenge the reverses which had been suffered by the French armies – led by the most experienced and able cavalry commanders – and they submitted to a heavy discipline ... [however] we were perfectly prepared and secure against its effects, so far as any military operation can be calculated upon.'[3]

LEFT: **The *Chasseurs à cheval* formed part of the Imperial Guard cavalry.** (Anne S.K. Brown Military Collection, Brown University Library)

The objective of this charge was to break the Allied line or at least to pin the Allied infantry down. In their static squares the Allied infantry would be easy targets for the French artillery and infantry which would be certain to be following the cavalry. But Ney did not bring any infantry or artillery forward. Instead, inexplicably, he ordered his cavalry to charge again.

Many of the Anglo-Netherlands battalions had been arranged in somewhat unusual oblong formations which were easily converted into squares or into line as the situation demanded. How this unusual formation worked was explained by Colonel James Stanhope of the 1st Foot Guards: 'When the cavalry attacked us in our squares (which they did with the most persevering gallantry, never retiring above 100 or 150 paces and charging again) our men ... changed from line to squares and from squares to lines, as the circumstances of the case required.'[4]

Mercer with his guns, meanwhile, had been moved to the front: 'Every man stood steadily at his post, the guns ready, loaded with a round shot first and a case over it; the tubes were in the vents; the port-fires glared and spluttered behind the wheels; and →

ABOVE: French cavalry charging a British square. Abandoned British artillery pieces can be seen in front of the square. (Anne S.K. Brown Military Collection, Brown University Library)

my word alone was wanting to hurl destruction on that goodly show of gallant men and noble horses. I delayed this, for experience had given me confidence ... It was indeed a grand and imposing spectacle. The column was led on this time by an officer in a rich uniform, his breast covered with decorations, whose earnest gesticulations were strangely contrasted with the solemn demeanour of those to whom they were addressed. I thus allowed them to advance unmolested until the head of the column might have been about fifty or sixty yards from us, and then gave the word "Fire!" The effect was terrible, nearly the whole leading rank fell at once; and the round shot, penetrating the column, carried confusion throughout its extent. The ground, already encumbered with victims of the struggle, became now almost impassable. Still, however, these devoted warriors struggled on, intent only on reaching us. The thing was impossible.'[5]

Death and Destruction

The situation inside the squares was horrifying. In the lull between charges the Grand Battery fired at the British squares and, when close enough, the French cavalry fired their pistols into the big blocks of infantry, impossible to miss. Some of the lancers, with their 2.7 metre-long weapons were able to reach beyond the bayonets of the Allied infantry to inflict further casualties.

'During the battle our squares presented a shocking sight,' continued Gronow. 'Inside we were nearly all suffocated by the smoke and smell of burnt cartridges. It was impossible to move a yard without treading upon a wounded comrade, or upon the bodies of the dead; and the groans of the wounded and dying was most appalling. At four o'clock our square was a perfect hospital, being full of dead, dying and mutilated soldiers.'[6]

The cavalry swept round the squares unable to break a single battalion. Lieutenant Colonel F.S. Tidy was in the square of his 3rd Battalion of the 14th Foot, as his daughter later related: 'After a slight pause, the cuirassiers made a sudden charge upon the regiment to the left of my father's, and after several attempts to break the square, they sounded a retreat, and retired in the utmost confusion. The attacked regiment waited only till the enemy was entirely clear of the 14th, when they opened upon them with a murderous fire, while at the same moment several guns on the other side of my father's corps played upon them. For a minute or two, the smoke was so dense, that it was impossible to see a yard in advance; but when it cleared away, a scene of the greatest disorder presented itself. Numbers lay strewed about in all directions, dead, dying and wounded. Horses running here and there without their riders, and the riders, encumbered with their heavy armour, scampered away as they best could, without their horses.'[7]

Nevertheless, it seemed inevitable that it was only a matter of time before the infantry's resolve began to crumble. Only one force was still in reserve to help the infantry, the Allied light cavalry. This included four British regiments, three King's German Legion, the Brunswick Hussars, the Hanoverian Cumberland Hussars, and seven Netherlands regiments. Altogether this amounted to an impressive 6,000 sabres. These, though, were all light cavalry, and regarded as inferior to Milhaud's cuirassiers and Lancers of the Guard. Uxbridge, however, did not hesitate to use his men, but he did not throw them recklessly into the action. Instead he placed them behind the squares, near enough for the infantry to feel reassured by their presence.

'Our brigade was then formed into line and there we stood showing them that we would have the ground or perish in the attempt,' declared Major General Hussey Vivan, the Brigade Major of the 6th Cavalry Brigade. 'But they did not much like our steady front.'[8]

The light cavalry did not just stand firm but actually engaged the enemy, as Joseph Sinclair of the 71st Highland Light Infantry saw: 'We stood in square for some time, whilst the 13th Dragoons and a squadron of French dragoons were engaged. The 13th Dragoons retiring to the rear of our column, we gave the French a volley, which put them to the right-about; then the 13th at them again. They did this for some time; we cheering the 13th, and feeling every blow they received. When a Frenchman fell, we shouted; and when one of the 13th, we groaned. We wished to join them, but were forced to stand in square.'[9]

Premature Attack

Supported in this way by Uxbridge's light cavalry, the infantry squares stood firm. Some of the light cavalry regiments even charged the French horse, but with varying degrees of success. One of these charges, by two squadrons, was witnessed by Major von Goeben of the 3rd Hussars King's German Legion: 'This attack was made, and that part of the enemy force that the two squadrons could reach was brought to a standstill and then violently thrown back. However, since the enemy line was so much stronger, these same squadrons were then outflanked on both sides and suffered a considerable loss in officers, men, and horses.'[10]

Strangely Napoleon, who we know for certain ordered Ney to carry out the charge of the cavalry,[11] claimed that

BELOW: A trio of magnificent French cuirassiers, represented by modern-day re-enactors.

LEFT: **By this stage of the battle casualties were very heavy. In the foreground of this image can be seen, in a dark dress coat, a mortally wounded General Picton, who commanded Wellington's reserve. Picton was the most senior Allied officer to be killed at Waterloo.** (Anne S.K. Brown Military Collection, Brown

the attack had been made prematurely, before the British were sufficiently softened-up by the Grand Battery. 'It is an hour too soon,' Napoleon said, 'nevertheless what has been done must be followed up ... it was important not to fall back at any point, and to hold the present position which the cavalry had taken, although it was premature.' Ney's 5,000 men had failed to break the Allies, but if even more cavalry were sent charging against the weakened infantry they might just win the battle.

The Emperor ordered General Kellermann's III Cavalry Corps, which had started the battle more than 3,700 strong, to support the cavalry swarming around the plateau of Mont St Jean. Napoleon watched as the cuirassiers, dragoons and carabineers jogged past. Behind Kellermann's squadrons, the Guard Heavy Cavalry Division moved into line in support.

Kellermann's men increased speed as they moved up the slope in front and, to Napoleon's astonishment, the Guard Heavy Cavalry Division, instead of remaining in reserve, followed Kellermann at full trot.

Napoleon sent General Bertrand to recall his Guard cavalry, but by the time he caught up with them the horsemen were already committed. 'From 5pm onwards,' complained Napoleon, 'I was thus deprived of my cavalry reserve, of that reserve which, skilfully employed, had so often brought me victory'.

The Imperial Guard Cavalry Division numbered just over 2,000 men. Coupled with Kellermann's cuirassiers and the regiments Ney had already led against the Allied line, this meant that around 10,000 cavalry now bore down on the infantry squares.

According to Napoleon these '12,000 [*sic*] picked cavalrymen performed miracles; they overwhelmed all the more numerous enemy cavalry which sought to oppose us, drove in several infantry squares, broke them up, seized sixty pieces of artillery, and, in the middle of the squares, captured ten standards, which three Chasseurs of the Guard and three cuirassiers presented to me in front of la Belle-Alliance'.[12] This was all fantasy.

None of the squares broke, not even the ill-trained Brunswickers and the Hanoverians and Belgians that had never been under fire before that day. They all held their nerve, and held their ground. All that throwing such large numbers of cavalry at solid infantry squares resulted in was even greater casualties.

'The [British] artillery did great execution, but our musketry did not at first seem to kill many men; though it brought down a large number of horses, and created indescribable confusion,' wrote Gronow. 'The horses of the first rank of cuirassiers, in spite of all the efforts of their riders, came to a stand-still, shaking and covered with foam, at about twenty yards distance from our squares, and generally resisted all attempts to force them to charge the line of serried steel.'

ABOVE: **The French 'Wounded Eagle' Monument at Waterloo, pictured during the 1920s. The memorial was unveiled on 28 June 1904 in front of a vast crowd estimated at 100,000. The Brussels railway station alone issued 57,000 tickets and many others travelled from elsewhere to witness the event.** (Historic Military Press)

The Cannonballs Fly

It was not, therefore, the French cavalry that the Allied infantry had to fear, but the French artillery was a different matter. Some guns of the Grand Battery, instead of remaining static, had manoeuvred so that they were able to see the Allied squares. Every time the French cavalry withdrew, the guns opened fire.

Captain von Sciba watched the effects of the French artillery: 'When the cannon fire recommenced, we were greatly distressed to see our neighbours to the right, the Nassauers, waver and fall into some disorder; but the efforts of the gallant Nassauer officers, who gave their subordinates an excellent example, succeeded in bringing the men to a halt and leading them back to their former places. This unfortunate incident was repeated once or twice, under identical circumstances. Their losses were quite considerable.'[13]

Ensign Leeke of the 52nd (Light Infantry) Regiment explained just how nerve-wracking it was to stand and watch the cannon balls flying towards them, unable to move or hide, and just how destructive they could be: 'The standing to be cannonaded, and having nothing else to do, is about the most

LEFT: **The British light cavalry being ordered to charge the French cavalry.** (Anne S.K. Brown Military Collection, Brown University Library)

RIGHT: A British light dragoon (right) in combat with a French dragoon. (Anne S.K. Brown Military Collection, Brown University Library)

BELOW RIGHT: The power of the artillery deployed at Waterloo, by both sides, is illustrated by the effects of a cannonball on this cuirass which was being worn at Waterloo on 18 June 1815. Now on display in the Musee de l'Armee in Paris, it belonged to a carabinier-à-cheval named François-Antoine Fauveau, a butter producer in civilian life. He was 23 years old at the time of his death. (Courtesy of World Imaging)

unpleasant thing that can happen to soldiers in an engagement ... I do not know exactly the rapidity with which the cannon-balls fly, but I think that two seconds elapsed from the time I saw this shot leave the gun until it struck the front face of the square [he was in]. It did not strike the four men in the rear of whom I was standing, but the poor fellows on their right. It was fired with some elevation, and struck the men in front about the knees, and coming to ground under the feet of the rear man of the four, who it severely wounded, it rose and, passing within an inch or two of the Colour pole ... The two men in the first and second rank fell outward. I fear they did not survive; the two others fell within the square.'[14]

In fact, the French artillery almost decided the day. 'I never heard yet of a battle in which everybody was killed,' remarked Johnny Kincaid of the 95th Rifles, 'but this seemed likely to be an exception, as all were going by turns'.[15]

It was almost a relief when the cavalry charged as it meant that the artillery had to cease firing. If it had been infantry that followed up the artillery bombardment the result might have been entirely different. Ney, of course, fully realised this and he sent a message to Napoleon asking for infantry support. The reply Napoleon sent back shows just how desperate the situation of the French had become: 'Infantry! And where do you expect me to find infantry? Do you expect me to manufacture some?'

Ney continued to lead the cavalry in charge after charge for more than two hours. They could do no more. The horses were blown, the riders exhausted and reduced to tears of frustration. The plateau beyond Mont St Jean ridge was littered with dead and wounded men and mounts. Ney himself, hatless, his uniform caked in mud and torn, his face black with gunpowder, was not one to give in but he could not ask his cavalry to charge the unbroken squares again.

It had been, as Wellington said during the battle, 'Hard pounding', but the squares had held. The situation was becoming increasingly critical for Napoleon. The great gamble of throwing almost his entire cavalry force at the Allied line had failed.

BELOW: French lancers of the Imperial Guard about to engage with British infantry. (Anne S.K. Brown Military Collection, Brown University Library)

NOTES:

1. W.H. Fitchett (Ed.), *Waterloo 1815 Captain Mercer's Journal* (Pen & Sword, Barnsley, 2012), p.92.
2. R.H. Gronow, *The Reminiscences and Recollections of Captain Gronow, being Anecdotes of the Camp, the Court, and the Clubs, and Society to the close of the last war with France*, (Nimmo, London, 1900), Vol.1, pp.69-72.
3. James Shaw Kennedy, *Notes on the Battle of Waterloo* (J. Murray, London, 1865), pp.115-6.
4. Gareth Glover (Ed.), *Eyewitness to the Peninsular War and the Battle of Waterloo, The Letters and Journals of Lieutenant Colonel The Honourable James Hamilton Stanhope 1803 to 1825* (Pen & Sword, Barnsley, 2010), p.184.
5. Mercer, *op. cit.*, p.101.
6. Gronow, *op. cit.*
7. Gareth Glover, *The Waterloo Archive* (Frontline, Barnsley, 2010), Vol.1, British Sources pp.169-70.
8. Glover, *The Waterloo Archive*, p. 89-90.
9. *A Soldier of the Seventy-First, From De La Plata to the Battle of Waterloo 1806-1815* [Edited by Stuart Reid], (Frontline, Barnsley, 2010), p.131.
10. Barbero, *The Battle*, pp.255-6.
11. We know this because Napoleon had issued an instruction on 16 June that General officers commanding corps 'will take orders directly from me when I am present in person'. When Ney ordered the cuirassiers to move up towards La Haye Sainte in preparation for the attack, General Delort, in charge of the 14th Cavalry Division, refused to accept orders from Ney unless they emanated from the Emperor. Delort sent an aide to Soult, Napoleon's Chief of Staff, who confirmed that Ney had indeed been given control of the cuirassiers. Hamilton-Williams, *op. cit.*, pp.320-1.
12. Napoleon Bonaparte, *The Waterloo Campaign* (The Folio Society, London, 1957), p.125.
13. Barbero, *op. cit.*, p.261.
14. W. Leeke, *History of Lord Seaton's Regiment at the Battle of Waterloo* (Hatchard, London, 1866), Vol.I, pp.30-1.
15. Kincaid, Sir John, *Adventures in the Rifle Brigade* (Thomas Nelson and Sons, London, 1907), p.224.

VISIT OUR ONLINE SHOP

shop.keypublishing.com/Dunkirk

KEY Shop

The operation to save the British Expeditionary Force from destruction, as Hitler's panzer divisions raced to the Channel coast, was on a scale unprecedented in history of warfare.

The story of the great evacuation is told, day-by-day, in this 100-page special publication in the words of those soldiers, sailors and airmen who fought and survived those dramatic nine days in the summer of 1940.

The operation that came to be known simply as 'Dunkirk' was born from what was referred to as the 'Phoney War' but ended with 300,000 men being saved to fight another day. It was the first step on the road to the ultimate victory.

ONLY £8·99 + FREE P&P*

SUBSCRIBERS don't forget to use your £2 OFF DISCOUNT CODE!

IF YOU ARE INTERESTED IN **WORLD WAR II** YOU MAY ALSO WANT TO ORDER...

£9·99

£8·99

£8·99

£5·00

FREE P&P* when you order online at...

shop.keypublishing.com/Dunkirk

Call +44 (0)1780 480404 *(Monday to Friday 9am-5.30pm GMT)*

Also available from **W.H Smith** and all leading newsagents.

467/23 **Free 2nd class P&P on all UK & BFPO orders. Overseas charges apply.*

'UP GUARDS AND AT 'EM'

After the battle, the British 1st Foot Guards were renamed the Grenadier Guards following their defeat of the Grenadiers of Napoleon's Old Guard. It is the name they proudly bear to this day.

MAIN PICTURE: The last stand of Napoleon's Old Guard. (Anne S.K. Brown Military Collection, Brown University Library)

BELOW: General Antoine, *comte* Drouot, commanded the entire Imperial Guard at Waterloo. (Anne S.K. Brown Military Collection, Brown University Library)

The Prussians were drawing closer. Bülow's Corps had appeared on the battlefield and the troops sent by Napoleon to hold it back, General Lobau's VI Corps and General Domon's Cavalry Division, had been forced to withdraw beyond the village of Plancenoit at the right rear of the French positions. Behind Bülow, the Prussian I Corps and II Corps were moving towards the French right flank. Unless Napoleon could do something spectacular, he would soon be swept away by the Prussians. With his cavalry weakened and exhausted by their attacks upon the British squares, Napoleon had only one body of men left – the infantry of the Imperial Guard.

Napoleon's Guard was like no other. At its peak it had reached a total of 35,000 infantry, 8,000 cavalry and 200 guns. Not all of its component regiments were considered elite, indeed many of the regiments that formed what was termed the Young Guard were often new recruits. The next in seniority were those regiments that formed the Middle Guard, with the Old Guard being the most prodigious in the army. Very high entry standards had to be met for entry into the Old Guard.

When he returned to power in 1815, Napoleon maintained these high standards. A minimum of 12 years service was required for the infantry of the Old Guard, and eight for the cavalry and artillery. All had to have served in several campaigns. Such was the quality of *l'Armée du nord*, for the Waterloo campaign even those that sought to serve in the Young Guard needed to have had a minimum of four years service.[1]

The Imperial Guard's reputation was second to none. Though Napoleon held the Old Guard back, only using it when necessary, everyone knew that when the Old Guard was called into the attack, it spelt the end for the enemy. That time had now come.

Napoleon sent General Duhesme with the Young Guard to stem the advance of the Prussians at Plancenoit. The Young Guard was heavily outnumbered but still it managed to recapture the village. As more and more Prussians marched on to the scene, the Young Guard found itself under intense pressure. Napoleon responded by sending in four battalions of the Old Guard – three of Grenadiers and one of Chasseurs. These few battalions managed to stabilize the situation, making Napoleon's right rear secure for the time being.

The Old Guard had bought Napoleon time, maybe just enough time, to beat Wellington and secure an astonishing victory. It was certainly the case that the French artillery had caused the Anglo-Dutch immense casualties and the attacks of the cavalry and of d'Erlon's infantry had further reduced the Allies' numbers and resolve. Now was the moment to unleash the rest of the Old and Middle Guard upon Wellington's thinning line.

The problem was that the sound of gunfire could be heard to the east. If the French troops knew that the Prussians were about to fall on their flank they might well refuse to commit themselves to an attack against the British. Napoleon knew this only too well, but he decided to us this to his advantage by telling his men that the gunfire heralded the arrival not of Blücher, but Grouchy!

He sent one of his aides to inform Ney of the appearance of Grouchy. *'Moniseur le Maréchal,'* exclaimed General Dejean, *'Vive l'Empereur! Voila Grouchy!'* Whether Ney believed it or not, he told one of his staff to go along the line and announce the good news to the troops.

Napoleon's ruse worked and the men cheered the Emperor, who put himself at their head to lead them forward as far as La Haye Sainte. Spearheading the attack of the Guard were five battalions, about 3,000 men, in battalion squares, formed in columns. These were the regiments of the Middle Guard, the 1/3rd, 2/3rd, and 4th Chasseurs and the 3rd and 4th Grenadiers. Baron Duchard's horse artillery had placed →

ABOVE: This painting supposedly depicts the moment when Wellington sees that the French are wavering and he orders the whole of his line forward for the first time in the day. (Anne S.K. Brown Military Collection, Brown University Library)

a two-gun team between each battalion. Behind the Middle Guard were about 1,500 men of the Old Guard, the 2nd Battalions of the 1st and 2nd Chasseurs and the 2nd Grenadiers. His most precious regiment, the two battalions of the 1st Grenadiers, remained in reserve.

Trumpets sounded the advance. The Guard marched forward, their drums beating the frantic drub, drub, drubbing of the *pas de charge*. The rhythm of their march was broken by the debris and detritus of battle – the dead, the dying, the broken guns and caissons. The smoke thickened, obscuring what lay ahead.

The Grand Battery fell silent as the Guard passed in front. Inspiring shouts of '*Vive l'Empereur*' were soon drowned by the roar of the Allied artillery, some 30 pieces of which discharged, first round shot then canister, double-charged for deadly close-range destruction.

The bodies of men and horses were so thickly strewn upon the ground, and the smoke of the guns so dense, that the French columns diverged from their original course, and from each other, with three of the battalions straying to the left.

Throughout the battle Wellington had kept his battalions in rectangular formations instead of the customary two-deep as it was easier for them to form square from this configuration. Even though they were about to be assailed by infantry, Wellington kept his line in their deep formations, but he now moved them forward from the rear of Mont St Jean onto the ridge itself.

Facing the Imperial Guard were the British brigades of Generals Adam, Maitland and Halkett, which by this stage of the battle probably numbered around 4,000 men, and the 3rd Netherlands Division, around 3,000 strong. 'The last attacking column made its appearance through the fog and smoke, which throughout the day lay thick on the ground,' related Major Kelly who was on the staff of General Maitland's Brigade. 'Their advance was as usual with the French, very noisy and evidently reluctant, the officers being in advance some yards cheering their men on.'[2]

The French columns came under fire from General Baron Chassé's 3rd Netherlands Division and three British batteries, plus the Dutch Horse Artillery Battery (*Batterij rijdende artillerie*) of *Kapitein* Carl Krahmer de Bichin which took up a position alongside the infantry and began firing canister at close quarters. This was described by Ensign Macready of the 30th Regiment: 'Some guns from the rear of our right poured in grape amongst them, and the slaughter was dreadful. Nowhere did I see carcasses so heaped upon each other ... they were served most gloriously, and their grand metallic bang, bang, bang, bang, with the rushing showers of grape that followed, were the most welcome sounds that ever struck my ears.'[3] Pounded by such an intensity of fire, the 1/3rd and 4th Grenadiers fell back.

The other French column was still intact and still advancing towards the Anglo-Netherlands line and towards Maitland's Guards Brigade, consisting of the 2nd and 3rd Battalions of the 1st Foot Guards. Maitland's men had been lying down under cover of the sunken lane, which was particularly deep at this point. Approaching them were the 1st and 2nd Battalions, 3rd *Régiment de Chasseurs*.

Wellington, who always seemed to be present at the most critical points, was with Maitland. Seeing that the decisive moment had arrived, he said, either 'Now, Maitland, now is your time!', or 'Up Guards and at 'em!' Whichever it was, the meaning was clear.

The Guards stood up at, at a distance of around 50 yards from the advancing French, levelled their muskets and, in Maitland's own words, opened fire 'with terrible effect'. Volley after volley at point-blank range tore into the French ranks and they inevitably fell back, at which moment the 1st Guards followed up with a bayonet charge.

The 1st Guards, in their enthusiasm, charged after the 3rd Chasseurs, only to rush into 4th Chasseurs who met them with a stunning volley. The shocked British Guards retreated back up the slope.

BOTH RIGHT: A Grenadier of the Guard and a Chasseur (in colour) of the Guard. Their uniforms and headdress are similar which is why it was thought at the time that it was just the Grenadiers who had been defeated by the 1st Guards and General Adam's battalions of the 52nd and 71st Regiments. Anne S.K. Brown Military Collection, Brown University Library)

LEFT: **A stylized depiction of the final moments of the Old Guard.** (Anne S.K. Brown Military Collection, Brown University Library)

BELOW LEFT: **General Pierre Jacques Étienne Cambronne commanded a brigade of the Chasseurs of the Guard. He always denied that he made either of the comments attributed to him concerning the Guard at the end of the battle.** (Anne S.K. Brown Military Collection, Brown University Library)

Once more the formidable battalions of the Imperial Guard, distinguished by their bobbing tall bearskins, marched up the gentle slope. It was then that one of Major General Frederick Adam's regiments, the 52nd (Oxfordshire) Regiment of Foot (Light Infantry), suddenly changed formation. Its commanding officer, Sir John Colborne, saw that his battalion outflanked the French column. He said to his adjutant, Lieutenant Winterbottom, 'We must bring the regiment up on the flank'. Winterbottom replied: 'We cannot do it, we cannot wheel the regiment.'

Colborne was not going to accept that as an answer and he insisted. 'Wheel the left company and the others will conform to it.'[4]

General Adam, seeing the 52nd changing formation, rode up to Colborne and asked him what he was doing. 'I am going to make that column feel our fire,' explained Colborne.[5] Fully appreciating what Colborne was doing, Adam rode off to bring up the 71st Foot (Highland Light Infantry) and the 95th Rifles to join the 52nd.

This was a bold move, as Captain John Cross of the 52nd later wrote that 'no one who was looking steadfastly at the movement of the Imperial Guards at that time, could say that the battle did not look critical, or, but the Imperial Guards had the appearance of success.'[6]

First of all Colborne sent one company of skirmishers to fire into the flank of the French column and to cover the movement of the rest of the battalion as it pivoted round. The 52nd was formed in two lines of half companies (platoons), the rear line at ten paces distance from the first. After giving three rousing huzzas, they followed the left company, passed along the front of the British Brigade of Guards in line and about 500 yards in front of them, almost forming an obtuse angle with them. By this time the →

BELOW: **Napoleon leaves the battlefield to escape in his carriage.** (Anne S.K. Brown Military Collection, Brown University Library)

RIGHT: Blücher seen here at La Belle Alliance as the British and Prussian troops meet up at the end of the battle. (Anne S.K. Brown Military Collection, Brown University Library)

52nd's line was almost parallel to the flank of the Imperial Guard columns. Now was the time, as Colborne had put it, to make the French feel the 52nd's fire.

A devastating volley was unleashed into the flank of the Middle Guard. This unexpected shock caused the French soldiers to hesitate. At first they were in some confusion, but then the left companies of the column turned round and began to return a heavy fire on the 52nd. This was a terrible mistake. The Guard, bayonets fixed, were supposed to sweep the British line away with cold steel and determination. By stopping to fire back at the 52nd, all momentum was lost.

ABOVE: The regiment that really turned the advancing tide of the Imperial Guard, the 52nd (Oxfordshire) Regiment of Foot (Light Infantry), in action during the final stages of the Battle of Waterloo.

The 4th Chasseurs tried to deploy into line but they were coming under an immense storm of musketry and canister from the Allied guns, 'the column waving, at each successive discharge, like standing corn blown by the wind'.

Incredibly, for ten minutes the Chasseurs held their ground until General Adam, seeing his brigade no longer threatened, moved across to support the 1st Guards, followed by General Colin Halkett's 5th Brigade. Fired upon from all sides, the Chasseurs' resolve broke. They turned and ran.

Seeing this, someone shouted the chilling words '*La Garde recule*'. The Guard had never been beaten before. No-one in the French army could ever imagine such a situation and the effect it had upon them was catastrophic. They knew it was the end.

Despite the efforts of the French generals, they could not keep their men in formation. Panic spread like lightning. With the sudden disintegration of the enemy, Wellington knew that the moment had come to finish them off. Standing up on his stirrups he took off his hat and waved his men forward.

The battle was undeniably lost but Napoleon still hoped to be able to rally his troops. There were still large numbers of garrison soldiers in France and if he could gain control of his troops it might yet be possible to prevent Wellington and Blücher from reaching Paris before he raised another army. He sent General Piré galloping off to Genappe to try and stem the rout, ordering his remaining Guard battalions to hold back the advancing Allies for as long as possible.

These last four Guard battalions – 1/2nd Grenadiers, 2/3rd Grenadiers, 2/1st Chasseurs, and 2/2nd Chasseurs – formed in square and retreating slowly along the road south, were soon engaged by Adam's and Halkett's brigades, Chassé's 3rd Netherlands Division and the light cavalry of Vivian and Vandeleur. The Old Guard's volleys kept the cavalry at bay, but the Allied infantry found the slow-moving squares an easy mark. Soon artillery was brought up and began to discharge canister into the midst of the squares. The squares rapidly shrank until they formed only triangles.

At this point one of the most famous episodes of the battle took place. Some British officers called on the Guard to surrender. They were answered by General Pierre Cambronne who was in the square of the 2/1st Chasseurs. There

RIGHT: General Graf von Bülow led the Prussian advance towards Waterloo. (Both above and right, Anne S.K. Brown Military Collection, Brown University Library)

are two versions of what his answer was. The first was a short expletive, 'Merde!' Almost five decades later, Victor Hugo, in Les Misérables, recorded Cambronne's reply as, '*La Garde meurt, elle ne se rend pas*' – the Guard dies, it does not surrender.[7]

Whichever comment was made, or possibly both, the answer was still the same, the Guard would not surrender. The result was the destruction of the four battalions.

Two squares of the Old Guard, within one of which was Napoleon, reached Rossomme intact. There, supported by a battery of Guard artillery, the Emperor tried to halt the tide of retreating Frenchmen, but they simply swept round the Guard battalions.

Seeing no hope of restoring order, Napoleon and his Old Guard headed for Genappe. There he found hundreds of abandoned carts, carriages and guns, the horses having been cut free and used by the fleeing troops to escape all the quicker.

Soon, though, the Prussians were bearing down on Genappe. After eight hours of hard fighting and having sustained heavy casualties, the Anglo-Netherlands army was in no condition to mount a vigorous pursuit. Not so the Prussians, who had only been engaged for the last few hours. It was Blücher's men that chased after the French. Napoleon, finally acknowledging that there was nothing more he could do, left for Paris.

'The arrival of the Prussian cavalry sweeping round to the right flank of the enemy, in masses with columns as far as the eye could reach,' observed Colonel Stanhope, 'was a magnificent spectacle'.

The Prussians had turned the tide of the battle. Until the Germans had appeared, bearing down upon the French right, the result of the battle had hung in the balance. But Marshal Blücher was able to write happily to his wife that, 'I have been true to my word. I was compelled to withdraw before superior forces; but on the 18th

acting with my friend Wellington, I have annihilated the army of Napoleon.'[8]

In July 1815 a Royal Proclamation declared that for their part in defeating the Grenadiers of the Imperial Guard, the 1st Foot Guards became the Grenadier Guards. It was a fitting tribute. The senior British infantry regiment had defeated the senior French regiment, and they took their name as a badge of honour – though this does not reveal the full story.

LEFT: Pictured in the 1920s, this monument to the Prussians is close to the village of Placenoit and was unveiled three years after the battle. (Historic Military Press)

FAR LEFT: The Prussian Monument today. It bears the following inscription in German: 'To our fallen heroes, in gratitude from King and Country. May they rest in peace. La Belle Alliance 1815.' The inscription is not surprising, for the Prussians wanted to call the Battle of Waterloo the Battle of La Belle Alliance because it was there that Blucher and Wellington met after the victory.

NOTES:

1. John Grehan, *The Age of Napoleon Army Guides, No.1 The French Imperial Guard*. (Partizan Press, Nottingham), p.55.
2. Quoted in Barbero, *op. cit*, p.360.
3. E.N. Macready, in *Colborne's United Service Magazine*, Vol.1 (1854), p.398
4. Ray Cusick, *Wellington's Rifles* (Pen & Sword, Barnsley, 2013), p.165.
5. Siborne, *Waterloo Letters*, p.284.
6. Quoted in Gareth Glover (Ed.), *Letters from the Battle of Waterloo: Unpublished Correspondence by Allied Officers from the Siborne Papers* (Greenhill Books, London, 2004), p.185.
7. Mark Adkin, *The Waterloo Companion* (Aurum Press, London, 2001), pp.418-9.
8. Hamilton-Williams, *op. cit*, p.339.

One of the many monuments to Wellington's victory which were erected throughout Britain. This stone obelisk was erected in 1818 by 'the ladies of Great Torrington' in North Devon to commemorate the Battle of Waterloo. (Courtesy of Neil Bond)

WAVRE
THE FORGOTTEN BATTLE

Napoleon had been beaten at Waterloo but the war was not over. Marshal Grouchy still faced the Prussians, knowing that if he was defeated he would be trapped in Belgium.

The rumbling thunder of the guns to the west told Marshal Grouchy that Napoleon was attacking the Anglo-Dutch forces at Waterloo. All Grouchy had to do was engage the Prussian Army and prevent it from joining that of Wellington. After their defeat at Ligny, Blücher's men had withdrawn to the town of Wavre on the River Dyle. At around 13.00 hours the advance units of General Exelmans' II Cavalry Corps made contact with the Prussian rearguard but Grouchy was not in a position to engage the Prussians with all his force until 15.00 hours.

With the bulk of the Prussian Army marching as fast as it could towards Waterloo to join Wellington, General Johann von Thielemann, with III Corps, was given the task of holding back Grouchy. The French marshal had around 33,000 men and 80 guns. Thielemann had just 17,000 men and 48 guns, but his position was a strong one.

The Dyle, normally a shallow stream at this time of the year and easily fordable, was in flood because of the torrential rain of the previous day. The town of Wavre extended for about half a mile along the left, or west, bank of the Dyle. It was connected with a few buildings, effectively a suburb of the town, on the eastern bank by two stone bridges, the larger of which carried the main Brussels-Namur road.

About three-quarters of a mile upstream, on the Wavre side of the river, was the Mill of Bierges, which was destined to be the scene of the fiercest fighting. Here there was a wooden bridge carrying a narrow country road. At Limal, a village two-and-a-half miles up-stream from Wavre, and at Limelette, another village a mile further on, there were further wooden bridges across the Dyle.[1]

All the buildings along the river had been hastily loop-holed by Thielemann's men and the two stone bridges had been strongly barricaded. Behind Wavre was a hill which could afford good cover for reserves and there were numerous lateral lanes along which troops could easily be moved to any threatened sector. →

MAIN PICTURE: British troops bivouacked in the Bois de Boulogne during the Allied occupation of Paris after the fall of Napoleon. (Anne S.K. Brown Military Collection, Brown University Library)

RIGHT: Napoleon's final act of abdication brought the Napoleonic Wars to a conclusion. (Anne S.K. Brown Military Collection, Brown University Library)

BOTTOM LEFT: A group of Prussian *Landwehr*. (Anne S.K. Brown Military Collection, Brown University Library)

BOTTOM RIGHT: An old photograph, of unknown provenance, showing the River Dyle at Wavre.

Thielemann placed his 10th and 11th divisions behind Wavre, with the 12th Division posted at Bierges, behind the village. The 9th Division was supposed to be the general reserve, but its commander, General Borcke, believing that III Corps was marching with Blücher, had set off to join the main army. By the time Thielemann was aware of Borcke's departure it was too late to call him back. The loss of Borcke's six battalions and accompanying artillery meant that Thielemann now had less than half as many men as Grouchy.

Pushing ahead in front of Exelmans' cavalry was General Vandamme with the French III Corps. He arrived in front of Wavre sometime between 15.00 hours and 16.00 hours. Anxious to prevent the Prussians from joining Wellington, Vandamme attacked Wavre without waiting either for the rest of the left wing to arrive and without even waiting for Grouchy.

Vandamme ordered his 10th Division to seize the main bridge across the Dyle, but every attempt to force the barricaded bridge failed, the French suffering terrible losses. As the attack broke up the men came under fire from the Prussian artillery posted on the hill behind the town. All the men could do was find shelter amongst the houses that lined the right bank.

At this point Grouchy arrived and, seeing that Vandamme was heavily engaged, supported him with attacks on either flank.

It was now 17.00 hours and it was at this time that he received Napoleon's order to march immediately to join the Emperor. But, with his forces engaged with the Prussians, this he simply could not do. The only way he could help Napoleon was to beat the Prussians at Wavre and then attack Blücher's main body before it could intervene at Waterloo.

Hulot's Division of Gérard's IV Corps was ordered to force a passage of the Dyle at the Mill of Bierges, led by Gérard himself. The attack was beaten back, with Gérard being badly

wounded. All, though, was not lost, as General Pajol's I Cavalry Corps had seized the bridge at Limal. The bridge was defended by three battalions of infantry and three squadrons of cavalry, but, quite unaccountably, had not been barricaded. Pajol sent a regiment of hussars charging across the bridge. So narrow was the bridge, the hussars could only gallop three abreast. They charged directly into the guns of the Prussian infantry and captured the vital bridge. At last the French were across the Dyle.

As soon as he realised that the river had been crossed, Thielemann sent all the troops he could spare to try and drive the French back over the Dyle. It was now dark, but the situation was so critical that neither side could afford to stop fighting. General Stulpnagel led the Prussian counter-attack. The ground, though, was unfamiliar to the Prussians and the darkness was intense so the attack soon lost cohesion and stuttered to a halt.

The confusion of the fighting in the darkness is well portrayed by the account of Second Lieutenant Mannkopff, who was in charge

of the skirmish platoon of the 4th Company of the 31st Regiment: 'We advanced with our skirmishers out in front and a long and determined battle broke out with the enemy voltigeurs in the darkness and amid the man-high corn that covered the fields. This soon became chaotically confused, with man fighting man. In this, my men and I had to face enemy voltigeurs and cavalry sometimes to our front, sometimes to our rear. About midnight, where possible, our skirmishers pulled back to the columns and a bayonet attack was made at the charge. However, because of the darkness and high corn, it was impossible to see and keep order …

'Meanwhile, my skirmishers had rejoined the battalion and during this attack suddenly stumbled into a deep sunken road or ditch. At that moment, a volley of small arms fire from the opposite side struck us. However, probably because the other side of the sunken road was higher, the shots mostly went over the heads of our soldiers and un-mounted officers, some of them making a loud rattling sound on hitting our bayonets. All our mounted officers were hit, though, including the regimental commander, Major von Kesteloot, and the battalion commander … Shortly after this bayonet charge, we broke off the battle and, without the enemy following up, withdrew to a pine forest close behind us.'[2]

The fighting also continued at Wavre and the Mill of Bierges. Thirteen times the French charged the barricaded bridges. Thirteen times they were beaten back. At one point Vandamme's men actually seized one of the bridges, but Prussian reserves were quickly brought up and the bridge recaptured before the French could consolidate their foothold.

Finally Thielemann ordered his men at Limal to pull back. He had achieved his goal of preventing Grouchy from interfering with Blücher's main body which had successfully defeated Napoleon.

Thielemann was still in close contact with the French, so close, in fact that the sentries on both sides could hear each other's movements. With no news from Waterloo, neither Grouchy nor Thielemann knew the outcome of the battle at Waterloo. Both, it is fair to say, believed that their side had won. Grouchy, in particular could not imagine that Napoleon could be beaten. What was absolutely certain was that the battle would resume in the morning.

Boney Beaten!

Battle was indeed rejoined at first light, the fighting beginning with a salvo from the French artillery. At some point, possibly as early as 06.00 hours, Thielemann received definite news of the result of the Battle of Waterloo and he galloped up to his men to tell of the great victory, as Lieutenant Mannkopff recalled: 'General Thielemann came up to us and said, "Children, yesterday a great battle between Napoleon and →

ABOVE: General Johann von Thielemann commanded the Prussian III Corps. (Anne S.K. Brown Military Collection, Brown University Library)

ABOVE LEFT: The uniform of a Prussian general officer in 1815. (Anne S.K. Brown Military Collection, Brown University Library)

LEFT: A forlorn Napoleon on board HMS *Bellerophon* on his way to exile on the Atlantic island of St Helena where he would remain until he died on 5 May 1821. (Anne S.K. Brown Military Collection, Brown University Library)

RIGHT: The so-called Waterloo Drum which can be seen in St Mary's Church at Orston, Nottinghamshire. An accompanying plaque states that 'this drum was used at the Battle of Waterloo June 18th 1815 and subsequently by the local village band'. (Courtesy of Alan Murray-Rust; www.geograph.org.uk)

ABOVE RIGHT: The British Waterloo Campaign Monument which is located in Cimetière de Bruxelles in nearby Evere. Designed by Jacques de Lalaing, below the monument is a crypt with 16 niches containing 17 bodies, which were transferred there between 1890 and 1894. Four of these were killed at Quatre Bras, the remainder at Waterloo.

Prince Blücher and Wellington took place. Napoleon has been totally defeated and is retreating. I have only just received this news, on my word. Now we have to stand firm and will soon receive support ..." Everyone was inspired by these words, and as if electrified, cried "Hurrah! Hurrah!" between the bursts of cannon fire.'[3]

The news inspired the Prussians and they drove the French backwards, re-gaining much ground. Believing that Grouchy must by this time be aware of Napoleon's defeat, Thielemann assumed that the French would now try to disengage. But Grouchy attacked with as much ferocity as before. The French marshal had still not heard from Waterloo and, it seems, just assumed that his Emperor had won.

Though Thielemann was puzzled by Grouchy's actions, he saw no point in continuing to fight and incur more casualties. He decided to disengage; knowing that at some point Grouchy would have to withdraw and try and escape back to Paris.

At 10.00 hours the Prussians began to pull back. Grouchy believed he had won the Battle of Wavre and was preparing to march on Brussels to meet up with Napoleon. Then, at around 10.30 hours, a messenger galloped up with the shocking news that the Emperor had been beaten.

Clearly Grouchy was in an extremely difficult position. Between him and the French border were the two victorious Allied armies. After consulting with his senior officers, he decided to withdraw to Namur. He sent Exelmans ahead to gain and hold the bridges across the Sambre, doing nothing further at Wavre to provoke Thielemann. During the night the French slipped quietly away.

Retreat

For obvious reasons, the movement of the various armies in the following days was called 'the race to Paris'. It was the Prussians, who had not been as heavily engaged on 18 June as the Anglo-Dutch army, who took up the pursuit of Napoleon. Blücher was determined to exact revenge and plunder from France and he drove his men headlong across the border, intending to force-march his

MAIN PICTURE: The Waterloo Trees on Wotton Hill, near Wotton-Under-Edge, Gloucestershire. The trees on this summit were originally planted in 1815 to commemorate the victory at Waterloo, though replacements have been added at various intervals in the years since. (Courtesy of Matthew Bigwood)

increasingly exhausted and ill-supplied men all the way to the French capital.

As for Grouchy, he still had a considerable body of men under his command and there was a possibility that Napoleon's broken force could rally around Grouchy and make a stand against the Allies. His objective, therefore, was to get back to Paris with his army in one piece as quickly as possible.

At Namur, Grouchy's men held off attacks by the leading units of Pirch's I Corps until, on the evening of the 20th, he marched off towards Dinant. The French blocked the bridges over the Meuse with stacks of burning wood, and so made good their escape.

On the 21st Grouchy, showing the kind of speed that evaded him earlier in the campaign, passed Dinant still ahead of Thielemann and Pirch, in his bid to reach Phillippeville. As they withdrew, Grouchy had his men barricade every narrow passage and place obstacles at intervals along the roads. Grouchy might have retired down the valley of the Meuse, instead of taking this more dangerous route where he would be liable to an attack in the flank. But he wanted to be as close to any of Napoleon's troops fleeing from Waterloo as he could.

It was on 25 June, when he arrived in Rethel, that Grouchy learnt that Napoleon had abdicated in favour of his son. There was no indication, however, that the war was over. A Provisional Government had been installed which sought an armistice with the Allies, but Blücher demanded the handing over of Napoleon, the surrender of Paris and control of all the fortresses on the Moselle, Meuse and Sambre. These terms were rejected and so the Prussians pushed on towards the French capital.

Grouchy then received a message directing him to march directly upon Paris, and shortly afterwards another message informed him that he was the supreme commander of all French forces in the north. The news of Napoleon's abdication led to a rapid decline in French morale and increasing numbers of Grouchy's men began to desert.

By 29 June Grouchy's force reached the line of fortifications defending the north of Paris. Having brought back his army largely intact, Grouchy considered his duty done and he resigned his position.

History, and in particular Napoleon, would loudly condemn Grouchy. In Napoleon's words, Grouchy 'accomplished the impossible, by being neither on the field of the battle of Mont Sainte Jean, nor at Wavre, during the day of the 18th'.[4] Napoleon had only himself to blame.

NOTES:

1. W. Hyde Kelly, *The Battle of Wavre and Grouchy's Retreat: The Right Wing of the French Army & Prussians during the Waterloo Campaign 1815* (Leonaur, 2010), p.73.
2. Peter Hofschröer, *1815 The Waterloo Campaign: The German Victory* (Greenhill, London, 1999), p.164.
3. *Ibid*, p.169.
4. Napoleon Bonapatre, *op. cit.*, p.156.

TOP LEFT: The imposing Waterloo Monument near Ancrum in the Scottish Borders. This 150 foot high tower was built between 1817 and 1824. Inside is a spiral staircase leading to the balcony which encircles the top of the tower. (Shutterstock)

TOP RIGHT: This French 6-pounder gun, cast in 1813 in Metz, can be seen today on display in the Tower of London.

THE WATERLOO DESPATCH

The great victory won, Wellington now had to sit down and write his official report. It was three days after the battle before the despatch reached London as the people of Britain waited with great anxiety for news.

It was early on Monday, 19 June 1815, when Wellington sat down in his headquarters in the little village of Waterloo to put into words all that had happened over the previous three days. When he had finished this most memorable account, and being left with few staff after the battle, Wellington rode to Brussels to have a fair copy of the document made. This copy was handed to the Duke's only aide-de-camp to survive the battle without injury, Major the Hon. Henry Percy.

At around midday Percy left Brussels for the coast in a post-chaise-and-four. Sticking out of the windows of the carriage were the gilded Eagles of the 45th and 105th Line captured by the Union Brigade. These would be laid at the feet of the Prince Regent.

Percy's first stop was at Ghent, before pushing on to Ostend where the 200-ton brig sloop HMS *Peruvian* lay. Percy joined *Peruvian* at 13.00 hours. Three hours later Captain White set sail. Normally a fast packet could cover the 60 miles or so to the UK in six or seven hours but, as White recorded in his ship's log, the winds were unusually light.

White sailed through the night but by 08.00 hours *Peruvian* was becalmed and still less than halfway to the British coast. One can imagine how Major Percy must have felt. Having been granted the honour of carrying the first news of one of the most momentous events in history, he was stuck in the middle of the Channel!

With little progress being made and Percy desperate to deliver the news for which the whole of Britain was waiting, the major and the captain abandoned the sloop and took to a gig. They were going to have to row the rest of the way.

With four strong tars, and all six men on the oars, they struck out for Dover, 38 miles away. Incredibly, it took them just four hours, if the journalist from the *Kentish Gazette* who published the details got his facts right.

They landed at around 15.00 hours on Wednesday 21st somewhere near Broadstairs, where Percy and White took another post-chaise-and-four and galloped for London. The chaise, with the Imperial Eagles poking through its windows, was cheered on through Kent, reaching the capital at about 22.00 hours as darkness descended upon the streets of London. →

MAIN PICTURE: This painting by David Wilkie depicts the moment that a group of Chelsea Pensioners received a copy of *The London Gazette* announcing the victory at the Battle of Waterloo. (Yale Center for British Art)

ABOVE: **At Stratfield Saye is the Duke of Wellington's impressive funeral carriage. The lower part was constructed from metal from French guns captured in 1815. Weighing 18 tons, it was completed in 18 days, a total of 100 men being employed in two shifts. It was drawn by 12 black draught houses, three abreast. After his death on 14 September 1852, the Duke lay in state in Chelsea Hospital for two days, during which period many thousands of mourners, including the Queen, paid their respects.** (Courtesy of Shani Thorpe; www.flickr.com/photos/shani1709)

RIGHT: **The place where Wellington wrote his despatch on the battle, in the village of Waterloo itself, is now a museum.**

The carriage clattered over Westminster Bridge, wheeled into Whitehall and turned into Downing Street, pulling up outside No.11 next to which were the offices of the Principal Secretary for the War Department, Lord Bathurst.

As it happened on this memorable day, Bathurst was at the Wednesday Cabinet dinner given by Lord Harrowby, the President of the Council, in his house in Grosvenor Square. Percy's coachman was directed there.

Harrowby's two young children were asleep on the top floor of the house when they were woken by the sound of men cheering. The two children crept to the landing and peered through the banisters. Mary Harrowby's account of what she saw was later recorded:

'An officer in a scarlet tunic with gold on it and brandishing the despatch came tearing into her father's house, followed by two other men, all asking for Lord Bathurst, and crying out "Victory ... Victory ... Bonaparte has been beaten ..." She saw Major Percy's face and noticed how tired and dishevelled he looked and watched him rush through the open door from the hall into the dining room, and a moment later heard renewed bursts of cheering from the men inside. Then her father, Lord Harrowby, came out, and standing outside the front door facing Grosvenor Square he announced the news to the great crowd who were pressing round the chaise and four, attracted by the sight of the captured French standards. In this dramatic yet informal way the first public announcement of the Battle of Waterloo was made from the door-step of No.44 Grosvenor Square.'

Percy had barely slept in the five days since he set off for the Duchess of Richmond's Ball on 16 June and he was on the verge of collapse. But he still had one more task to perform.

The Prince Regent was also at dinner, with his brother the Duke of York, in nearby St James Square. They were the guests of Mr and Mrs Boeham, a wealthy merchant and his wife.

The Prince had opened the ball and the first dance was about to start when cheering from outside could be heard over the music. The dancers rushed to the windows, which were flung open to reveal a crowd of people waving and cheering. Through the crowd galloped a chaise and four which pulled up outside the house.

Out jumped Percy, the staff of an Eagle clutched in each hand. He dashed into the house and up the stairs to the ballroom. Seeing the Prince, Major Percy strode across the floor. Bending down on one knee, he repeated the news of the great victory and presented the Prince with the Eagles and Wellington's Waterloo despatch.

'Wellington! Victory!'

Mrs Harriet Ward, the daughter of Lieutenant Colonel Frank Tidy who was in command of the 14th Foot under Wellington, wrote about how the news of the battle reached her family in England: 'My mother anxiously awaited news from the Continent. It came at last – and in this way; for she, having little intercourse with anyone beyond her children, had scarcely any knowledge of what was passing in the world abroad. My brother and I, standing at the front gate of the cottage garden, were one morning attracted by the sound of music, and the gaudy appearances of the coaches coming down the road, streaming with gilded flags that bore the words –WELLINGTON! VICTORY! WATERLOO!

'These words, in printed capitals, caught our eyes. We repeated them with the passing crowd, and then rushed into my mother. "There has been a battle," we said; "they have been fighting the French, and *we* have beaten them!"

'My mother started up, and without bonnet or shawl was proceeding to the post-town, about two miles from where we were residing, when her maid followed her through the gate with these necessary articles. She put them on mechanically, and hastened on her road. She has often said, she knew not how she reached the post-office; but she got there safely, and received two letters – one from my father containing but few words. They had gained the victory; he was safe, but his favourite mare had been shot under him …'

Mrs Tidy returned to the cottage and sat down with her family in the porch. 'On a low chair sat my mother, with her little ones gathered round her,' continued Harriet. 'My father's letter was in her hand, and she was reading it aloud. A faithful servant, with one of the children in her arms, stood beside her; while we, silent and wondering, gazed and listened earnestly. The golden sun streamed up the garden-walk, and shed its light upon our little group: bees murmured in the jasmine porch, and the perfume of June flowers came floating through the open door.' Wellington had won the day, and life was good.

Praise To The Victor

Official recognition for Wellington was quick in coming. The Prince Regent wrote on 22 June, the day after the Waterloo despatch had arrived: 'I lose not a moment in communicating to you the fullness of my joy and admiration at the unparalleled triumph of your last and greatest achievement. Greatest, my dear Lord, not only in military glory, but in political importance; and not only in this proof of what all believed, that even the consummate skill of the Corsican could not withstand the superior genius of our own hero, but in the now realised expectation, resulting from this victor, that England, under the auspices of her transcendent General, is again destined to rescue the world from tyranny and oppression.'

In the House of Lords the following day, 'Earl Bathurst rose, pursuant to the notice which he had given, to move the Thanks of the House to the Duke of Wellington, and the Army under his command, for those transcendant exertions which led to the victory of the 18th of this month. He was aware that their lordships must be eager to discharge the debt of gratitude to the Duke of Wellington, who had now so gloriously opened the campaign, and relieved them from the anxiety which all must have felt for some time past. However sanguine any of them might have been as to the final result, yet there were none who must not have experienced the utmost anxiety with respect to the turn which the campaign might take at the commencement.'

Earl Bathurst's announcement ended thus: 'He had now, then, only to move their lordships, That the Thanks of this House be given to Field Marshal the Duke of Wellington, Knight of the most noble Order of the Garter, for the consummate ability, unexampled exertion, and irresistible ardour displayed by him on the 18th of June, on which day the decisive victory over the enemy, commanded by Buonaparté in person, was obtained by his grace, with the Allied troops under his command, and in conjunction with the troops under the command of Marshal Prince Blucher, whereby the military glory of the British nation has been exalted, and the territory of his Majesty's ally the King of the Netherlands, has been protected from invasion and spoil.'

As well as the vote of thanks, Wellington received £61,000 prize money for the victory at Waterloo, a far greater amount than was given to the others who fought during the campaign. General officers received just £1,274 10s 10¾d, Field officers and colonels were granted £433 2s 4½d; captains got £90 7s 3¾; Subalterns £34 14s 9½d; Sergeants £19 4s 4d; and lowly corporals, drummers and privates received just £2 11s 4d, their only reward for having won history's greatest battle.

The Casualties

In his despatch, Wellington provided this "Return of the Killed, Wounded, and Missing of the British and Hanoverian Army".

In the battle fought at Quatre Bras on 16 June 1815:

Killed;	Officers, 29,	Serjeants, 19,	Rank and File, 302.
Wounded;	Officers, 126,	Serjeants, 111,	Rank and File, 2,143.
Missing;	Officers, 4,	Serjeants, 6;	Rank and File, 171.

On the retreat from Quatre Bras to Waterloo, 17 June 1815:

Killed;	Officers, 1,	Serjeants, 1,	Rank and File, 33.
Wounded;	Officers, 7,	Serjeants, 13,	Rank and File, 112.
Missing;	Officers, 4,	Serjeants, 3,	Rank and File, 64.

In the battle fought at Waterloo, 18 June 1815:

Killed;	Officers, 116,	Serjeants, 109,	Rank and File, 1,822.
Wounded;	Officers, 504,	Serjeants, 364,	Rank and File, 6,148.
Missing;	Officers, 20,	Serjeants, 29,	Rank and File, 1,574.

ABOVE: The Wellington Memorial at the entrance to Stratfield Saye House. This commemorative column was erected in 1863. (Shutterstock)

LEFT: The vote of thanks to Wellington came with something more substantial as he was also granted £200,000 'for the purpose of building and furnishing a house fit for the residence of the Duke of Wellington'. That house was Stratfield Saye in Hampshire, which, duly modernised and extended by Wellington, remains the home of the Dukes of Wellington to this day. (Shutterstock)

'A Grateful and Admiring Country'

The significance of Waterloo was not lost on the British public and the Duke of Wellington sought to reward all those who had participated in such an epoch-changing campaign, with the issue of a medal.

MAIN PICTURE: The obverse and reverse of the Waterloo Medal. (Historic Military Press)

The Battle of Waterloo was possibly the single most important event of the nineteenth century. Though many of the nations of Europe subsequently struggled to maintain their integrity against internal rupture, 18 June 1815 was the last time that the great European powers faced each other on the battlefield for almost 40 years.

The suggestion to award a decoration marked a change from tradition in which only officers were awarded medals. After some debate it was agreed that the medal would be made of the same metal for all ranks and would be the same size and design regardless of whether the recipient was a general or the lowliest private. The medal would also be issued to those regiments that had been involved in all three days fighting of the campaign as well as those that formed the reserve at Hal, i.e. the 33rd, 54th, 59th and 91st, and the two brigades of the Royal Artillery. Such was Wellington's influence that any suggestion by him was tantamount to an instruction and the idea was quickly accepted by the Government and the Prince Regent.

The task was handed to the Royal Mint with several designs being prepared by Thomas Wyon. Despite a serious fire at the Royal Mint and the fact that the original decision to make the medals out of bronze changed half-way through the process to silver, the Master of the Mint, William Wellesley Pole, was able to write the following on 4 March 1816:

'The Medals which I received His Royal Highness the Prince Regent's pleasure to strike, for the Officers and Men who fought at the Battle of Waterloo, have been some time in preparation, and those for the General and Staff Officers are now ready for delivery. I propose packing the Medals in Boxes marked on the outside so as to specify the Corps or Regiment to which the Medals within may belong; and there will be packed in each Box a copy of the List transmitted from the Horse Guards, which copy will be certified by the Principal Officers of the Royal Mint.

'The Medals are all fitted with Rings, and a quarter of a yard of Ribbon for each will be packed in the Boxes. The Name of each Officer and Man, who is to receive a Medal, is impressed upon the edge of the Medal destined for him, and care will be taken to pack the Medals in the order in which the Names stand on the several Lists. The number of names, including Officers and Men, which have been transmitted from the Horse Guards to the Mint amount to more than 35,000; and I am in hopes that we shall be enabled to deliver finished Medals, packed as I have already mentioned, at the rate of about 1,000 per day from this time forward until the whole are completed.

'Each Medal contains one ounce of Fine Silver, intrinsically worth, at the present market price of Bullion, about six shillings. There is no difference whatever in the quality, figure or workmanship, between the Medals for the Officers and those intended for the Soldiers.'

The final version was one-and-three-eighth's-of-an-inch in diameter and struck in fine silver. The design on the obverse was of a laureated bust of the Prince Regent facing left, with the legend GEORGE P. REGENT. The reverse, meanwhile, carries the figure of Victory, with outspread wings, seated on a cippus, holding in her right hand a palm branch and in her left an olive branch. On the base or platform is the word WATERLOO, above which is WELLINGTON; below is JUNE 18. 1815.

Thomas Wyon engraved the portrait of the Prince Regent from a drawing by Sir Thomas Lawrence, whilst the figure of Victory was taken from one of the Greek coins held in the British Museum. The coin itself was selected by Mr Pole, who had seen the coin in the collection of Sir Richard Paine.

The edge of each Waterloo Medal is stamped, incuse, with the rank, name, and regiment of the recipient. In another first, this stamping was done by machine. The suspender consists of a large common split key-ring, which is attached to the medal by a steel clip. It was worn with a red ribbon, one-and-a-half-inches wide, with blue borders, the colours being the same as those issued with the gold medals and crosses for the Peninsular War. →

R. REGENT
WELLINGTON
WATERLOO
JUNE 18.
1815

ABOVE:
A contemporary drawing entitled 'Cost of a Waterloo Medal'. The French hussar on the left is deriding the Waterloo Medal, saying that it cost only two francs. In reply the British infantryman responds: 'That's true. But it cost yours a Napoleon', referring to the French gold coin.
(Anne S.K. Brown Military Collection, Brown University)

BELOW RIGHT:
The Waterloo Medal of Captain T.N. Quicke, who led a Troop of the 1st King's Dragoon Guards as part of the famous charge of the Heavy Cavalry, the Household and Union Brigades. His regiment suffered over 50% casualties during the course of the campaign, also losing its commanding officer in the charge. The medal was sold by Spink for £11,000 at auction in 2008.
(Courtesy of Spink; www.spink.com)

The issue of the Waterloo Medal was announced in *The London Gazette* of 23 April 1816: 'The Prince Regent has been graciously pleased, in the name and on the behalf of His Majesty, to command, that, in commemoration of the brilliant and decisive victory of Waterloo, a medal shall be conferred upon every Officer, Non-Commissioned Officer, and Soldier of the British Army present upon that memorable occasion. His Royal Highness has further been pleased to command, that the ribband issued with the medal shall never be worn, but with the medal suspended to it.'

Altogether, a total of some 39,000 medals was struck by the Royal Mint. Of this number, 6,000 were issued to the cavalry, 4,000 to the Guards, 16,000 to the infantry, 5,000 to the artillery, 6,500 to the King's German Legion and 1,500 to miscellaneous units, attachments

and others. The first instalment was reported by the Mint as being ready for delivery on 4 March 1816.

The medals continued to be issued throughout 1816 and 1817. Not only was the Waterloo Medal the first campaign medal awarded to all ranks, it was also the first medal awarded to the next-of-kin of men killed in action. As well as the award of the medal, recipients were also credited with two extra years' service and pay.

The names of all those who were awarded the campaign medal were recorded in the Waterloo Medal Roll. This is a large leather-bound, hand-written volume, with the names of the soldiers entered under their regiments. A copy of the Roll is held by the Royal Mint Museum. The volume in the Royal Mint Museum is of especial interest because of the supplementary pages appended at the end. These pages, extending into the 1830s, contain the names of additional troops to whom the medal was awarded some years after the battle for reasons relating to late claims or the loss of an original medal.

The medals were soon being distributed amid great public celebration, as this description in the *Derby Mercury* of Thursday, 11 April 1816, reveals:

'The corps of Scotch Greys, at present stationed in Canterbury, were drawn out in the Barrack Field on Monday last, and to those who were present at the battle of Waterloo, a silver medal was presented to commemorate their gallantry in that well-fought field. The medals, to the number of 313, were alike distributed to the officers and men, and are to be worn on all occasions; they are about the size of a three-shilling bank token; on one side is a fine likeness of the *Regent*, on the other *Fame*, with a wreath of *Victory* above the figure of *Wellington* – under *Waterloo*, while on the exergue, is stamped the name of each man whose valour entitled him to this honourable distinction, from a grateful and admiring country. The whole army is to partake of this honour.'

A few days later, it was the turn of the men of the 23rd Regiment of Light Dragoons. This account of the presentation ceremony, written by reporter for the *Morning Post*, was published on Friday, 30 May 1816:

'Last Sunday we witnessed a grand, interesting and gratifying Military Spectacle, at Radspole Barracks, that

THE NASSAU MEDAL

Duke Friedrich of Nassau also distributed a Waterloo medal to all of his troops present at the battle. Seen here, this was in silver with the Duke's image on the obverse, with the reverse showing the winged figure of Victory crowning a soldier with laurels, below which was the date of the struggle.
In December 1817, the Prince Regent, as guardian to the young Duke of Brunswick following his father's death at Quatre Bras, instituted a 'Brunswick' Waterloo Medal which was to be issued to all the Brunswick troops present in the Waterloo campaign. Pressed in bronze, this had an image of the Duke on the obverse and on the reverse was a wreath of laurel and oak leaves enclosing the German text *'Braunschweig Seinen Kriegern'* (Brunswick to its warriors) and the words 'Quatre Bras' and 'Waterloo'.
(Courtesy of Spink; www.spink.com)

imposed on the feelings of every one present the most reverential awe. It being the period appointed that Lieut.-Colonel CUTCLIFFE read the commands of his Royal Highness the Commander-in-Chief, previous to his distributing the honourable Medals to that part of the 23d Regiment of Light Dragoons which so nobly distinguished itself at the ever-memorable Battle of Waterloo, on the 18th of last June ...

'In the morning the troops paraded as usual for Divine Service; after which, the ranks were opened to receive those inestimable badges of distinction.

'The guard, which formed on the right of the regiment, wheeled to the left; the Standard-bearers, together with the Troop Sergeant-Majors, formed in their front; the latter for the purpose of carrying the Medals of their respective Troops, which were laid on separate silver salvers ...

'Their distribution being completed, Lieut.-Colonel CUTCLIFFE addressed the Regiment in very eloquent, animated, and appropriate terms; at the conclusion of which, the vociferations and heartfelt acclamations of the whole Regiment were heard at a great distance, and repeated by a very respectable assemblage of visitants and inhabitants.'

Understandably, the Waterloo Medal soon gained a worth over its intrinsic value, as this report in the *Morning Post* of Saturday, 14 September 1816, reveals: 'Samuel Wise, a private in the 25th Dragoons, charged Charles Macfarland, a seaman, with robbing him of his Waterloo Medal. Prisoner, on being asked who he was, and what he had to say, informed the Magistrate that he had lately been the mate of a merchant ship arrived from the West Indies, but at present resided with his brother, who is a pilot and ship-owner, at Shadwell, and that he meant the whole as a joke.

'Mr Fielding asked the Prosecutor, if, on his oath, he had conceived [the] Prisoner's conduct to be a joke? He [Wise] answered that, for a full hour or more, he really did, but after his persisting in it so long, and he saw him [Macfarland] drawing towards the door, he began to fear Prisoner meant to carry the joke too far and rob him of his medal.' The Magistrate obviously agreed with Private Wise, for the report ended by noting that Macfarland was remanded in custody.

On Tuesday, 29 December 1818, the same newspaper detailed the circumstances surrounding the theft of another Waterloo Medal on Saturday, 26 December 1818. The defendant on this occasion was one John Wilson: 'James Markwick, a private belonging to the 2nd Battalion, 3rd Regiment of Foot Guards, which were lying in the Tower, stated that on Saturday night last he was passing through Rosemary-lane when the Prisoner snatched at his breast and stole his silver Waterloo Medal, with which he ran off. Witness immediately cried "stop thief", and the Prisoner was stopped by the watchman.' Wilson was also remanded in custody.

The interest in this campaign medal has not lessened with the passage of time. Indeed, one of the highest prices ever realised at auction by a single example relates to that awarded to the next of kin of Major (and Lt Col) Samuel Ferrior, 1st Life Guards, sold by the specialist auctioneers Spink. Ferrior, who was killed in action while in command of his regiment on 18 June 1815, was 'said to have lead his regiment to the charge no less than 11 times, and most of the charges were not made till after his head had been laid open by the cut of a sabre and his body was pierced with a lance'.

Despite a pre-sale guide price of £14,000 to £18,000, Ferrior's campaign medal sold for £33,000. Such is the draw of the Waterloo Medal.

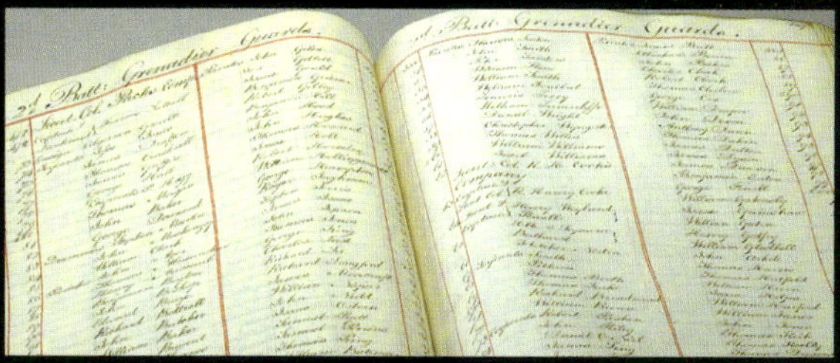

ABOVE: The Waterloo Medal Roll records the name of every recipient of the campaign decoration.

BELOW LEFT: The Waterloo Medal awarded to Major (and Lieutenant-Colonel) Samuel Ferrior. (Courtesy of Spink; www.spink.com)

THE HANOVERIAN MEDAL

Like the British medal, this award was struck in silver and was worn with the same clip, ring, and riband. On the obverse was a laureated bust of the Prince Regent, this time looking to the right, with the legend, GEORG PRINZ REGENT 1815. The reverse had two laurel branches enclosing the words WATERLOO JUN XVIII, above which was a trophy of arms. The obverse bore the legend HANNOVERSCHER TAPFERKEIT. The edge of the medal was stamped with rank, name, and regiment of the recipient, in the same fashion as the British medal. Another medal issued to commemorate the battle was instituted by King George III on 12 August 1815 to reward his Hanoverian subjects. This was the Order of the Guelph, and there was both a military and civilian division, each of which consisted of three classes, namely, Grand Crosses, Commanders, and Knights. There was also a medal called the Guelph Medal, issued to non-commissioned officers and soldiers who had distinguished themselves in the fighting. Though the intention was that the Order of the Guelph would be for Hanoverians, it was largely bestowed upon British subjects.

(Historic Military Press)

THE LAST REDCOAT

The remains of a soldier dating back to the time of Waterloo were unearthed during the excavation of land for a car park close to the Lion Mound monument. Who might he be?

MAIN PICTURE: The body of one of the fallen from the Battle of Waterloo which was found during preparation work for the 200th anniversary. (© Dominique Bosquet, SPW-DG04)

The remarkable discovery of a virtually intact skeleton during work to extend car parking facilities ahead of the 200th centenary of the battle prsented archaeologists and historians with a challenging puzzle. With all of the soldier's uniform except for a small piece of leather having corroded completely, there were no obvious indicators to help establish his identity. There were, though, a few other clues.

Possibly the most revealing element was the discovery of a musket ball amid the bones of his rib cage. Though the left foot is missing and the left leg is clearly broken, we do not know when this damage occurred, so it is safe to assume that he was shot through the chest. It is likely, however, that he was not fatally wounded where his remains were discovered, as they were found to the rear of the Anglo-Netherlands line closer to where the main surgery was located at Ferme Mont St Jean. The conclusion drawn is that he was hit and dragged away from the Mont St Jean to the rear, where he then died. There was probably nothing that the surgeons could do for him even if he reached the operating table alive.

RIGHT: Burying the fallen at Waterloo. This was a slightly romanticized image of the burial of the dead. An eye-witness recorded what actually took place: 'The general burying was truly horrible – large square holes were dug about six feet deep, and thirty or forty young fellows, stripped to their skins were thrown into each.' (Courtesy of Extraordinary Editions)

Speaking of the unearthing of the body, Yves Van Der Cruysen, director of the Battle of Waterloo Association, said: 'This is a major discovery. It is the first time for over a hundred years that a complete corpse of a combatant from the time has been discovered in such a good state. The body clearly has not been robbed as we found money on him, including a half franc coin from 1811 … He could have been buried by a comrade or simply missed when the bodies were gathered up after the battle for burial.'

RIGHT: The part of the Waterloo battlefield where the body was unearthed. (© Dominique Bosquet, SPW-DG04)

Identification Clues

So was this the skeleton of a British redcoat, a blue-frocked Frenchman, or a black-clad Brunswicker? The first clue that archaeologists have noted is that with the skeleton was a piece of wood inscribed with the initials 'C.B.' It has been suggested, because of its shape, that this might be the remains of the butt of his musket. If so, then this implies that he was an infantryman. As the bulk of the forces on both sides were infantry, this is a fairly safe assumption anyway.

The second piece of evidence comes in the form of the calibre of the musket ball, and this has been found to be French. While a so-called 'friendly fire' incident cannot be completely ruled out, it is considered improbable. Our poor infantryman is almost certainly a member of Wellington's army, and this is reinforced by the fact that he was found at the rear of the Anglo-Netherlands positions.

The other significant find with the body was a collection of coins which, over time, have corroded and become strongly bonded together. In total there were 22 coins, ten of which have now been restored as far as possible by Cristel Capucci and Marie-Hélèn Schmacher of Archaeology Services of the Brabant Walloon Province.

Though some of these coins are too badly corroded for any identifying marks to be read, others have provided valuable information. One of the coins is Austrian, three are from Hanover and five were minted in Paris.

Diverse though these are, they explain much. Firstly they are unlikely to have belonged to a British soldier, who would have possessed at least some of his own country's currency. Secondly, no Austrian troops were present at the battle.

Monetary Anarchy

That someone should possess such a mixture of coins is easily understood, if a little complicated to explain. The upheavals of the French Revolution led to what has been called 'monetary anarchy', with foreign currency and counterfeited coins circulating alongside the old Royal coinage. After Napoleon seized power in 1799, as First Consul he tried to bring matters back under control by issuing the 'germinal' franc named after the month Germinal in the Revolutionary calendar. →

FAR RIGHT: The musket ball pictured where it was found – in the victim's rib cage. (© Dominique Bosquet, SPW-DG04)

BELOW RIGHT: One of the coins found with the soldier's remains, pictured after cleaning and conservation. (© Dominique Bosquet, SPW-DG04)

BOTTOM LEFT: The initials 'C.B.' carved into the piece of wood, possibly a rifle butt, which was found beside the body. (© Dominique Bosquet, SPW-DG04)

BOTTOM RIGHT: This large spoon was found lying next to the engraved piece of wood beside the skeleton. (© Dominique Bosquet, SPW-DG04)

THE LAST WITNESS

In January 1904, *The Sphere* newspaper printed a story about Elizabeth Watkins (neé Gale) who, it was claimed, was the last surviving witness of the Battle of Waterloo. Mary, who was born on 31 January 1810, followed her father whom, she believed, swallowed the King's shilling at the bottom of a pint pot, to the Continent. She described her father's uniform as bottle-green with dark trousers – no doubt a rifleman. 'While the guns were thundering in the neighbourhood of Hougomont, Plachenoit and Mont St Jean little Elizabeth Gale sat by her mother's side shredding lint and helped some of the women rudely dress the wounded soldiers,' ran the article. 'She has a vivid recollection of several men dying in the camp and was much frightened when her mother lifted a cloth which covered the face of one of them and she saw the dead man's eyes apparently staring vacuously towards the battlefield.' Mrs Watkins died sometime in 1904 and it was believed that with her passing, the last person to have witnessed the Battle of Waterloo had gone.

As it transpired this might not have been the case. *The New York Times* published the following on 16 July 1905. 'Last Saturday we announced that there was a survivor of Waterloo but a little while ago. John Vaughan is still alive, and he was a bugler in the great fight. "I saw him at Walsall Railway Station two months ago," writes a correspondent, "and had a conversation with him, in the course of which he told me he was born at Aldershot, March, 1801." He can walk well enough, but two wounds in the left leg make help necessary when it comes to getting into a railway carriage. He sells bootlaces, as we said, for the veteran finds he cannot live on his country's gratitude, which comes to seven shillings a week. Surely we might do a little better than that for John Vaughan!'

It was decreed that the new franc would replace all the previous currencies and that this would form the basis of future transactions.

Such an objective was easier to decree than to put into practice. Not only would it take a long time to mint the numbers of coins required, but also people were not willing just to throw away their other coins. So the French administration had to permit the old coins to remain in circulation.

As the French Empire expanded, this confused coinage inevitably followed and a mixture of coins could be found tendered in the markets of the occupied countries. Belgium and The Netherlands were among those countries that came under French rule and in 1803 Hanover was invaded. The collection of coins found around the pelvis/femur area of the unearthed casualty's remains (indicating that they were in his pocket when he died) suggest, therefore, that this particular individual was probably either from the United Kingdom of the Netherlands or Hanover.

The Last Redcoat

We can narrow a possible identity down even further. In 1807, Napoleon created the Kingdom of Westphalia for his brother Jérôme. It was a collection of various states including some of the territories of Hanover. Among his first acts, Jérôme ordered that the French monetary system should be adopted throughout the new kingdom. This proved highly unpopular and he was forced to continue striking the old coins as well as bringing in the new francs. It means that pfennigs and francs circulated together. It is just such a combination that was found among the coins of the skeleton. Our unknown warrior was, almost certainly, Hanoverian.

While some of the Hanoverian infantry at Waterloo wore green uniforms, some wore red. So the soldier uncovered near the Lion Mound might well be the last redcoat from the Battle of Waterloo.

MODEL VICTORY

When a vast scale model of the battle was constructed it included thousands of Prussian figures close to the centre of the action. Wellington insisted that the model was inaccurate and a bitter struggle ensued, one that Wellington was determined to win.

It was decided in 1829 that London should have a military museum to rival the great museum at Les Invalides in Paris. The centre-piece of the new United Services Museum would be a vast scale model of the Battle of Waterloo. The job of building the model was entrusted to Lieutenant William Siborne whose two books *Instructions for Civil and Military Surveyors in Topographical Plan-drawing* and *A Practical Treatise on Topographical Surveying and Drawing* marked him out as ideal for the task. He was commissioned by the then Commander-in-Chief of the British Army, General Rowland Hill, Wellington at that time having devoted himself to politics.

Such an important construction, that would be seen by thousands and thousands of people and minutely scrutinized by those that had fought at the battle, needed to be as accurate as possible. Siborne had not been present at the battle so he spent eight months surveying and studying the battlefield, living as a guest at the farm of La Haye Sainte.

Siborne returned to Dublin, where he was the assistant military secretary to the Commander-in-Chief, Ireland, and began to create his model of the battlefield. He chose for the horizontal scale, that of nine feet, or 108 inches, to the mile, roughly 1:600; and approximately 1:180 for the vertical scale. To populate the model, each figure represented two actual soldiers. This meant that 80,000 figures had to be crafted and authentically painted.

As the troops were constantly on the move during the battle Siborne decided to pick one particular moment to portray in his model – a snapshot in time. The moment he chose was what was defined as the 'Crisis of the Battle' at around 19.00 hours, as the Imperial Guard reached the crest of Mont St Jean.

Wellington, who became Commander-in-Chief of the Army for a second time in 1842 after his spell in politics, was not happy with this. His stated reason was that if Siborne 'went to one gentleman and said, "What did you do?" [he would reply] "I did so and so." To another, "What did you do?" [and he would also reply] "I did such and such a thing." One did it at ten and another at twelve, and they have mixed up the whole. The fact is, a battle is like a ball; they keep footing it all the day through.' Wellington believed that Siborne should have chosen the start of the battle for his model as the exact position of all the troops was beyond doubt at that stage.

Not appreciating the consequences of his subsequent decision to ignore Wellington's opinion, Siborne persisted with re-creating the 'Crisis'. In order to be able to place every regiment in exactly its correct position at that moment in time, Siborne received permission to write to every surviving officer. He had been advised simply to use Wellington's despatch as his guide, but Siborne felt he needed more detailed information. Yet he did not see that there would be any conflict with Wellington's despatch and he stated that he would not place a single figure on the model without the great man's consent. However, there had been a change of government since Siborne had been commissioned to start the model and the new administration refused funding. Having started, Siborne was determined to finish the project, using his own money. →

MAIN PICTURE: **A general view of Captain H.T. Siborne's impressive model on display at the National Army Museum in London. The model was completed in Ireland in 1838 and shipped to England in 39 sections. For more information on a visit to the museum, see: www.nam.ac.uk** (Courtesy of the National Army Museum)

LEFT: **Siborne's depiction of the French attack upon Hougoumont. The orchard is to the left side of the wood that surrounds the farm buildings.** (Courtesy of the National Army Museum)

RIGHT: **The attack upon the Allied centre on Mont St Jean.** (Courtesy of the National Army Museum)

BELOW LEFT: **Just a few of the many thousands of model soldiers that can be found on Siborne's diorama.** (Courtesy of the National Army Museum)

BOTTOM: **A panorama of the Waterloo battlefield as it appears today from the top of the Lion Mound (see the next chapter). The village of Waterloo itself is to the left, the community of Brain-L'Alleud to the right.**

It is worth reproducing, at this point, the relevant part of Wellington's despatch concerning the moment Siborne had chosen to represent: 'The enemy repeatedly charged our infantry with his cavalry, but these attacks were uniformly unsuccessful ... These attacks were repeated till about seven in the evening, when the enemy made a desperate effort with cavalry and infantry, supported by the fire of artillery, to force our left centre, near the farm of La Haye Sainte, which, after a severe contest, was defeated; and, having observed that the troops retired from this attack in great confusion, and that the march of General Bülow's corps, by Frischermont, upon Planchenois and La Belle Alliance, had begun to take effect ... and as Marshal Prince Blücher had joined in person with a corps of his army to the left of our line by Ohain, I determined to attack the enemy, and immediately advanced the whole line of infantry, supported by the cavalry and artillery. The attack succeeded in every point: the enemy was forced from his positions on the heights, and fled in the utmost confusion.'

Wellington had made it clear that the Prussians had made no significant contribution to the fighting until the end of the battle, by which time the French were already beaten. In the 20-odd years that had elapsed since the battle, Wellington's version of events had been the accepted one. The Duke of Wellington, twice Prime Minister and Commander-in-Chief of the Army, was widely regarded as the greatest living Briton. His integrity was beyond question. If Wellington said that was what happened on 18 June 1815, then that was what happened.

Siborne, though, was gradually reaching a somewhat different conclusion. He had sent out his circular asking the officers where their units had been at about 19.00 hours, what enemy formations were to their front and for any further comments they would like to make about the parts played by their regiments. He appended a plan of the battlefield and asked the officers if they could mark the positions of their own and the enemy's units on it.

In total Siborne received around 700 replies and gradually assembled the most comprehensive collection of eye-witness accounts of the battle. As the replies came in, Siborne amended the position of the relevant regiments on a map. If the information in one letter contradicted that of another, Siborne went to considerable lengths to resolve the discrepancy. Finally after some three years he was ready to complete the positioning of his figures.

Unfortunately what the model showed was that the Prussians, far from being scarcely involved in the action at the time of the 'Crisis', were in fact on the battlefield in large numbers. By 19.00 hours, 49,886 Prussians with 123 guns were in action.

This contradicted Wellington's despatch. The silent figures on the model landscape loudly challenged the great man's veracity. It was even claimed by von Müffling that when Wellington stood on his stirrups and ordered his men forward he did so for reasons other than tactical ones. 'The Duke, with his practised eye, perceived that the French army was no longer dangerous; he was equally aware, indeed, that with his infantry so diminished he could achieve nothing more of importance; but if he *stood still*, and resigned the pursuit to the Prussian army *alone*, it might appear, in the eyes of Europe, as if the English army had defended themselves bravely indeed, but that the Prussians alone decided and won the battle.'

In October 1838 the 'Model of the Battle of Waterloo' went on display at the Egyptian Hall, Piccadilly. 'No fewer than 160,000 figures are represented,' declared a report in the *Morning Post* of 5 October, 'and with so much accuracy that not only the nation, but the very branch of the service to which they belong, is perfectly obvious on the nearer points; while the more distant points are distinctly marked out by the various lines of fire, distinguished as they are by representation of smoke, as ingenious as it is efficient. The roads and enclosures – nay the different appearance of wood, corn fields, or fallows – are all presented to the eye in the most natural manner; and if evidence be required of the correctness of this *charte vivante*, we can offer that of our own observations made on the spot in the last few weeks.'

The model proved to be an immediate success, with around 100,000 people paying 1 shilling each to view it. One person who was conspicuous by his absence, however, was the Duke of Wellington.

Despite the model's popularity Siborne received little money from the man who put it on display and Siborne, who had spent thousands of pounds on its construction,

faced the sad prospect of having to sell the model to recoup his losses. Severely short of funds, Siborne even volunteered to change the model in any way that a purchaser might require. He was prepared to sacrifice all the years of painstaking effort to ensure the model's accuracy rather than face a debtor's court.

He even wrote to the Army and the Government for help in preserving the model, but he knew that one major obstacle stood in his way.

Siborne was well aware of Wellington's disapproval of the moment in time that he had chosen to represent, and he knew that he had contradicted Wellington's despatch so, with his creditors closing in, he felt that he had no choice but to re-arrange the figures on the model to fit Wellington's version of events in the hope that he would therefore receive some official backing. The only way he could do that was by moving the Prussians further from the action to indicate that they arrived on the battlefield far later than had been established by Siborne. But, limited by the scope of the model, this actually meant completely removing the equivalent of 40,000 Prussians from the model.

Siborne now, though, had to justify his decision to remove the figures. He could not dare say it was because of pressure from Wellington and the Establishment, as that would only inflame the situation. Instead he did this through the medium of a book on the Waterloo campaign he had decided to write based on all the knowledge he had accumulated. This book, *History of the Waterloo Campaign*, was first published in June 1844. It was, and remained for a very long time, the most accurate and detailed history of the campaign. It sold in large numbers and over 170 years later it is still in print.

The publication of the book gave Siborne the opportunity to explain why he had removed the Prussians from his model. Stating that because of 'the evidence I had collected ... was of too vague a nature, as regards *time* and *situation* [Siborne's italics] to enable me either to corroborate or to rectify the details with which I had been furnished by the Prussian authorities'. He concluded that 'according to the *original* [Siborne's italics once again] arrangement of the figures upon the model, the Prussian troops distributed along that intervening space, immediately in front of Lobau's corps, were represented in too forward a position'.

Siborne then went even further in his bid to placate Wellington by writing: 'It was only subsequently, when collecting that further information which has enabled me in this present work to describe with such minuteness of detail those brilliant dispositions of the Duke of Wellington, by which he not only defeated the French imperial guard upon his position, but secured the victory.'

All this, however, did him no good. He had earlier cast aspersions on Wellington's honour and he would never be forgiven. 'It is curious,' the Duke wrote, 'that the Historian of the Battle of Waterloo, Captain Siborne, having discovered that in his capacity of artist he had failed in producing an accurate, and even intelligible, representation of the Battle of Waterloo, on his beautiful and accurate model of the ground, by having listened to every hero of his own tale ... the consequences of which have been to render ridiculous and useless that beautiful work ... while he lays aside and unnoticed the authentic [*sic*] reports by the General Commanding-in-Chief.'

So that was it. Wellington's version of the Battle of Waterloo remained the only one, confirmed by none other than William Siborne, the man who created the magnificent model and wrote the standard history of the campaign. So it has remained ever since. Few still dare to consider that Wellington had misrepresented the facts to reflect his greater glory.

The model remains in the care of the National Army Museum - including the large areas of empty terrain!

Acknowledgement: *With the exception of the comments made by Baron von Müffling, which are taken from his earlier-mentioned memoirs, the above story has been drawn almost exclusively from Peter Hofschröer's brilliant investigation into the history of the Siborne model,* Wellington's Smallest Victory, *which was published by Faber and Faber Limited of London in 2004. A copy of the circular sent to officers can be found in H.T. Siborne's* Waterloo Letters *along with many of the replies he received. The remaining letters were recently published by Gareth Glover in his book* Letters from the Battle of Waterloo, *which was published by Greenhill Books in 2004.*

ABOVE LEFT: **The Prussians advancing through the hamlet of Frischermont to fall on the French right flank.** (Courtesy of the National Army Museum)

ABOVE RIGHT: **Another spectacular representation of the Battle of Waterloo is the panorama which can be found at Waterloo itself. More correctly known as a cyclorama, this visual representation was created in 1912 by artist Louis Dumoulin and is 360 feet long and 39 feet high. The canvas, last restored in 2008 and now enhanced by quadraphonic sound, is housed in the original building erected for that purpose in 1912 – the circular structure seen here. It is located next to the Waterloo visitors centre.** (Shutterstock)

RUINATION OF A BATTLEFIELD

One of the highlights of a visit to Waterloo is climbing the Lion Mound from where the whole battlefield can be viewed. However, its construction fundamentally changed the nature of the ground upon which the battle was fought.

MAIN PICTURE: The Lion Mound at Waterloo which towers over the battlefield. (Zheng Huang/ Shutterstock)

Through the smoke and the bullets Napoleon's Imperial Guard moved ever closer to the Anglo-Allied line. The relentless advance of the Guard was too much for Halkett's brigade which broke and ran. Such was the disorder amongst the ranks of Halkett's men, one of his officers later wrote, that '50 cuirassiers would have annihilated our brigade'. The reason why the French failed to take advantage of this potentially disastrous gap in the line was because of the Hereditary Prince of Orange.

The Prince was the only officer left on horseback and he responded quickly. He unsheathed his sword and, putting himself at the head of one of Colonel von Kruse's Nassau battalions, led them directly towards the column of the 1/3rd Grenadiers of the Imperial Guard. This sudden counter-attack caused the Grenadiers to halt momentarily. It was just long enough for Halkett and his officers to rally the brigade. It was one of the most crucial moments of the battle. The Prince, however, had been wounded in the shoulder almost as soon he had led the Nassauers forward. It was only with difficulty that his aides persuaded him to retire and be treated.

As a tribute to his son's courage, King William I of the United Netherlands decided, in 1820, to build a monument on, or near, the spot where the Prince was wounded. Work began three years later led by the Dutch Royal Architect, Charles Van der Straeren. It was an enormous undertaking for the time and well over ten million cubic feet of earth was used. Unfortunately, the earth was taken from between La Haye Sainte farm and the former sunken road that ran east to west from Ohain village along the front of the Anglo-Dutch position.

A visitor to Waterloo as the mound was being constructed wrote to *The Times* of 28 October 1823: 'There is a double carriage road winding round it, in a spiral form, and supplying an easy means of ascent for carriages to the very top; and by this road the materials have been, and are, conveyed to complete the work.

LEFT: **The Prince of Orange leads his men against the Imperial Guard just before he was wounded.** (Anne S.K. Brown Military Collection, Brown University Library)

MIDDLE LEFT (OPPOSITE PAGE): **The Lion Mound during its construction. It took some 2,000 workers to build the mound, employing 600 horses and countless carts. It is said that many of the labourers who worked on the mound were *bot'resses liègeoises*, women who normally worked in the Liège coal mines.** (John Grehan)

'In the centre is a shaft of brick-work, which has been carried up from the bottom, and is still going on. It is to be 60 feet higher than the top of the mound … At present, as the works are going on, at the top it has a pleasing appearance, from the great number of horses, carts, and people ascending and descending by the winding road.'

The mound is actually 42.5 metres high with the circumference of the base being 518 metres. The lion on the top faces defiantly south – towards France. Because of the lack of roads at the time, the pieces of the lion were transported from Liège by boat to Dordrecht in Holland then via the estuary of the Scheldt and the Willebroek canal to Brussels harbour. From there they were taken by a wagon drawn by 20 horses to Mont St Jean and each piece taken to the summit to be assembled.[1]

The Lion Mound, or *Butte du Lion* in French and *Leeuw van Waterloo* in Dutch, was completed in 1825. The lion was placed looking proudly towards France, which angered many of the French. One night at the start of the 20th century the pedestal was painted in the French national colours of blue, white and red. On another occasion an individual, clearly one of Napoleon's supporters, wrote on the monument: 'Here treason triumphed by chance. Instead of this lion, there should be a fox.'

Even after the First World War, the defiant pose of the lion still rankled with the French. In the summer of 1919 a French socialist deputy, a Monsieur Pepin, actually asked the Belgian Government to turn the lion round to face to towards the north in recognition of the French role in liberating Belgium from the Germans.

Others were unhappy with way the battlefield had been altered by the building of the Lion Mound, as Victor Hugo explained in his famous book *Les Miserables*. As a Frenchman he was dismayed at the way the Mont St Jean had been reduced by the removal of so much earth, as it then appeared that the slope was insignificant. The sunken road, where the British Guards had sheltered, had also disappeared: 'Everyone is aware that the variously inclined undulations of the plains, where the engagement between Napoleon and Wellington took place, are no longer what they were on June 18, 1815. By taking from this mournful field the wherewithal to make a monument to it, its real

BELOW: **The Prince of Orange holds a piece of material to the wound in his left shoulder.** (Anne S.K. Brown Military Collection, Brown University Library)

RIGHT: **The Lion Mound in the 1920s. Note the sheer number of visitors gathered on the viewing area around the summit.** (Historic Military Press)

CENTRE: **The lion that stands on the Mound's summit, to represent both Belgium and Britain, was cast in nine separate pieces at the Cockerill works in Liège. It weighs 28 tons, is 4.4 metres high and 4.6 metres long, and stands on a 4.6-metre high stone pedestal.** (Historic Military Press)

BELOW: **Visitors to the Lion Mound, like those of the previous two centuries, complete the climb to the summit of the Lion Mound to take advantage of the stunning views that it provides of the Waterloo Battlefield.** (Sergey Dzyuba/Shutterstock)

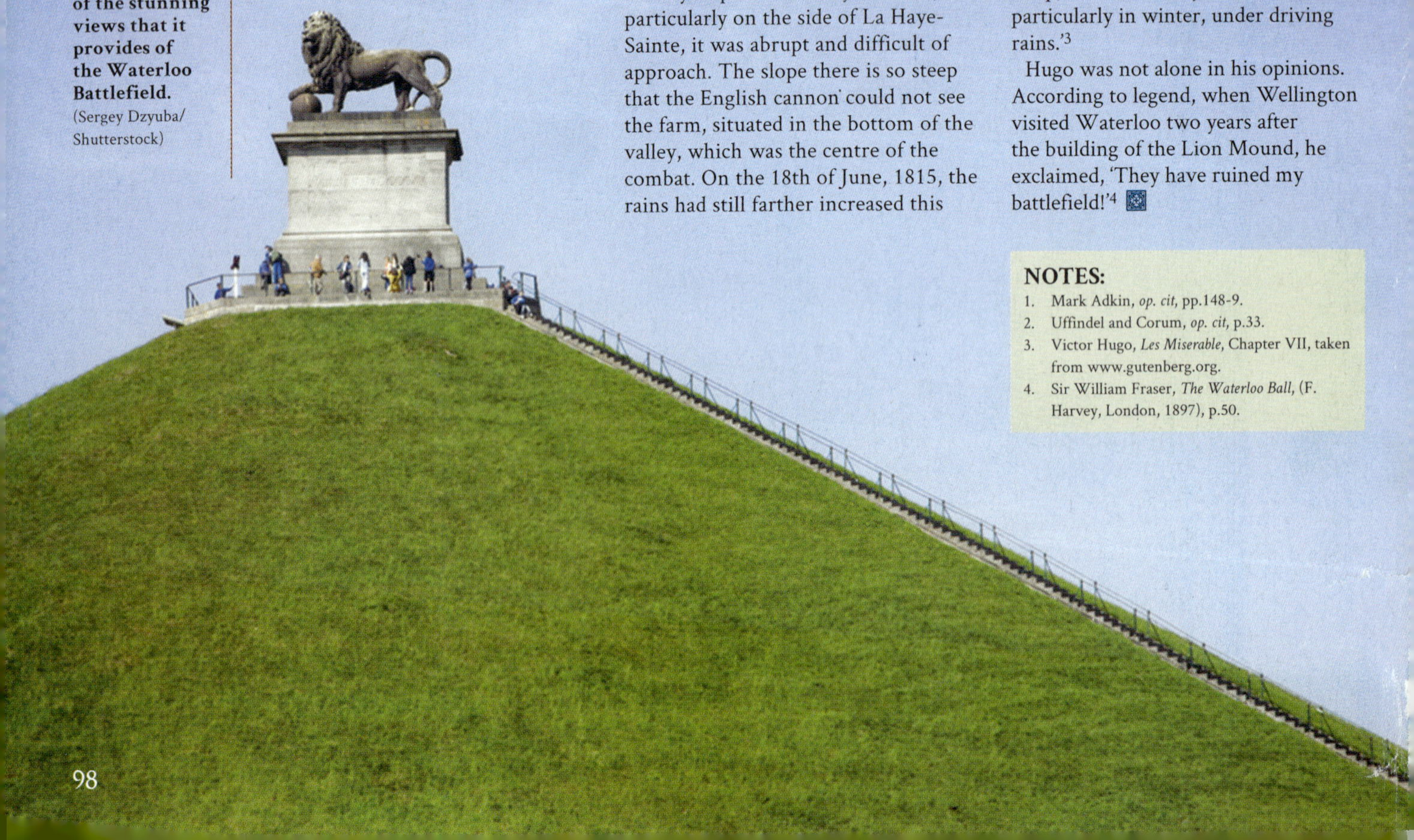

relief has been taken away, and history, disconcerted, no longer finds her bearings there. It has been disfigured for the sake of glorifying it ... Where the great pyramid of earth, surmounted by the lion, rises to-day, there was a hillock which descended in an easy slope towards the Nivelles road, but which was almost an escarpment on the side of the highway to Genappe. The elevation of this escarpment can still be measured by the height of the two knolls of the two great sepulchres which enclose the road from Genappe to Brussels: one, the English tomb, is on the left; the other, the German tomb, is on the right. There is no French tomb. The whole of that plain is a sepulchre for France. Thanks to the thousands upon thousands of cartloads of earth employed in the hillock 150 feet in height and half a mile in circumference, the plateau of Mont-Saint-Jean is now accessible by an easy slope. On the day of battle, particularly on the side of La Haye-Sainte, it was abrupt and difficult of approach. The slope there is so steep that the English cannon could not see the farm, situated in the bottom of the valley, which was the centre of the combat. On the 18th of June, 1815, the rains had still farther increased this acclivity, the mud complicated the problem of the ascent, and the men not only slipped back, but stuck fast in the mire. Along the crest of the plateau ran a sort of trench whose presence it was impossible for the distant observer to divine.'

The trench Hugo refers to is the sunken road, which he then goes on to describe. 'In 1815, as at the present day, this road cut the crest of the plateau of Mont-Saint-Jean between the two highways from Genappe and Nivelles; only, it is now on a level with the plain; it was then a hollow way. Its two slopes have been appropriated for the monumental hillock. This road was, and still is, a trench throughout the greater portion of its course; a hollow trench, sometimes a dozen feet in depth, and whose banks, being too steep, crumbled away here and there, particularly in winter, under driving rains.'[3]

Hugo was not alone in his opinions. According to legend, when Wellington visited Waterloo two years after the building of the Lion Mound, he exclaimed, 'They have ruined my battlefield!'[4]

NOTES:

1. Mark Adkin, *op. cit*, pp.148-9.
2. Uffindel and Corum, *op. cit*, p.33.
3. Victor Hugo, *Les Miserable*, Chapter VII, taken from www.gutenberg.org.
4. Sir William Fraser, *The Waterloo Ball*, (F. Harvey, London, 1897), p.50.